Adopters On Adoption
Reflections on parenthood
and children

Acknowledgements

First and foremost, I must thank the many parents of adopted children who so willingly gave of their time. Their experience, insight and wisdom helped me understand and appreciate so much of the process and practice of adoption. I met and spoke with so many warm, kind and extremely thoughtful people, the research was a constant pleasure and privilege.

Diana Hinings of the University of East Anglia helped with several of the interviews. Her knowledge of adoption matters is extensive and I benefitted greatly from our many conversations together. The Nuffield Foundation's Small Grants helped pay for some of the travelling expenses associated with the research and their support is gratefully acknowledged. And finally, Shaila Shah, Hedi Argent and Jude Tavanyar read the manuscript in its draft stage and made many helpful and useful comments which saved me from making too many errors of fact and judgement. I should like to thank them for their time, expertise and diligence. However, any failings or faults that remain are entirely mine for which I must take full responsibility.

David Howe
Norwich

Adopters on Adoption

Reflections on parenthood
and children

David Howe

B r i t i s h

A g e n c i e s

f o r **A** d o p t i o n

a n d **F** o s t e r i n g

Published by
British Agencies for Adoption & Fostering
(BAAF)
Skyline House
200 Union Street
London SE1 0LX
Charity registration 275689

© David Howe 1996

British Library Cataloguing in Publication Data
A catalogue record for this book is available
from the British Library

ISBN 1 873868 32 4

Designed by Andrew Haig & Associates
Typeset by Avon Dataset Ltd, Bidford on Avon
Printed by Russell Press (TU), Nottingham

Contents

1 Adopters and their families

It is now commonplace to observe that the character of adoption has changed radically over recent years. However, the more astute commentators also point out that the changing nature of adoption has always mirrored the changing nature of society. Adoption, its meaning and practice never stand still. For different generations and different cultures, the weight given to the needs of parents on the one hand and the needs of children on the other have expressed themselves in a range of adoption practices. Securing heirs, making family alliances, consolidating community relationships, caring for orphans, meeting the needs of childless couples, and meeting the needs of disadvantaged children have been some of the many reasons for practising adoption in different times and different places.

Adoption has also held a fascination for people both inside and outside the adoption experience. The movement of children between families and parents seems to trigger deep concerns about origins, identity and relationships. To whom do we belong? To whom are we related? Who, in terms of close relationships, are we?

Adoption, too, is defined by other, equally powerful themes in human experience to do with love and reproduction, loss and separation, care and compassion. Little wonder it is so often the subject of novels, plays, films and documentaries. How does it feel to "lose" one's parents? What is it like to raise another woman's child as one's own? How do adopters and their children relate to the birth mother – the woman who voluntarily relinquished or legally forfeited her right to raise her child? Behind these questions lies yet another layer of intrigue and interest to do with the power of genes versus the impact of environment on our development. What is the balance of influence between a child's inherited characteristics and the way he or she is raised? How does love fare in the face of biology? These, of course, are questions of fundamental interest not only to detached scientists but also to the adopters and their children.

Most developmental psychologists now recognise that in practice there is a complex interaction between nature and nurture, between our natural temperamental make up and the social world in which we happen to find ourselves. Natural predispositions can affect the way other people react to us just as much as other people can influence the way we behave and feel about ourselves (see *Developing Minds* by Michael and Marjorie Rutter,[1] for a good introduction to many of these issues).

There have been two significant changes in adoption philosophy and practice over the last twenty years or so. The first witnessed a shift from seeing adoption as a way of meeting the needs of childless couples to thinking about adoption as a method of giving children the best developmental opportunities. Naturally, these two perspectives happily combined in many instances, but the change of view did represent a major switch in child care philosophy. The needs and well-being of children are now the touchstones upon which all decisions and plans are made. The needs of both adopters and biological parents are secondary.

The second change has seen a huge drop in the number of babies needing to be adopted and a rise in the placement of older children. Two separate social trends explain this change. Improved contraception, the legal availability of abortion, changing social attitudes and better financial support have meant that fewer babies have been put forward for adoption. There has also been a rise in the belief that older children, often with a variety of "special needs," were in fact adoptable. Many families were willing and able to take these so-called "hard-to-place" children, the majority of whom were coming from poorer families via the public care system.

There is one other change in the type of child being adopted that needs to be noted. Though not as widespread as, say, in countries like Sweden or Germany, there has been a steady increase in the number of children being adopted from overseas – usually poorer, "third-world" countries.

Changes in the type of children being adopted have undoubtedly led to major changes in the character of adoption. The ideas and practices that supported the adoption of babies were not always suitable for dealing with older children. Children who had previously been in foster care or residential homes usually have a history of neglect or abuse or some kind of incompetent parenting. Such experiences of loss, separation and harm cause upset and psychological disturbance. In the cases of older children, they will also have memories – sometimes good, sometimes bad – of mothers, fathers, brothers and sisters. Adopting these children can be a very different matter to adopting a one week old baby. Nevertheless, adoption specialists set about placing these children in optimistic mood, believing that no child is unadoptable and that adverse experiences and psychological damage can be overcome by judicious parenting.

However, some of the real difficulties in parenting children whose psychological development had been upset or disturbed soon forced people to modify their initial outbursts of unqualified optimism. It was realised that early deprivations *did* affect emotional development and that raising some of these children was by no means easy. Although older adopted children nearly always benefitted from joining a new family, it was less certain whether all new families benefitted from adopting an older child.

One of the unexpected consequences of these various changes in practice was to force people to think about the nature of adoption. In particular, the adoption of older children made people realise that in many key respects, adopting children *is* different to having children by birth. For a long time, the argument was that adoption was, and should be, practised and experienced the *same* as biological parenting. Adoptive parenting and biological parenting were regarded as "equivalent". Although people were beginning to suspect the strength and wisdom of this notion, it did seem to have particular merit if children were adopted as babies. But with the findings of research and the reports of adopters and their children, people began to realise that in certain respects, adopting and being adopted were different to being biological parents and birth children. There were psychological and developmental tasks that all adopted children and their families had to negotiate if they were to adjust successfully to their special experience. These tasks are to do with loss and separation, identity and belonging. Adopted children have to work out what adoption means to them and other people in order to work out who they are, both to themselves and others. To this extent, according to David Brodzinsky,[2] an American psychologist, there is a psychological risk in being adopted. If parents and children are able to

3

negotiate these tasks well, then in terms of their development, adopted children do, indeed, end up as strong as birth children raised in similar families.

However, if the children arrive in their new families already adversely affected by poor quality experiences, they may not have the psychological strengths to deal as well with their developmental tasks as their more robust, adopted baby counterparts. To this extent, adopting older children (who may be as young as a year or less in age at the time of placement) who have been neglected or abused, means that not only do parents have to cope with the disturbances resulting from the poor quality of their pre-placement care, they also have to deal with children who are less able to negotiate the normal but extra developmental tasks that all adopted children have to manage.

It has also been increasingly recognised that the children's biological parents, particularly their birth mothers, continue to be "psychologically" present in the minds of many children and adoptive parents. The birth mother, therefore, cannot be ignored. Her continued existence has to be acknowledged in one way or another. This is particularly true if the adopted child has memories of the birth mother. The growing trend for more open adoptions with some kind of contact with birth parents (whether by occasional letter, exchange of photographs or even personal visits) is an attempt to build in some of these understandings into adoption practice.

The net impact of all these social changes, research findings and shifts in philosophy has been to produce a much more complex picture of adoption. Adopting and being adopted remains a relevant factor in parent–child relationships throughout life, whether spoken or unspoken. Adoption is still a highly successful and appropriate practice in the field of child welfare and wellbeing. Literally millions of people throughout the world have benefitted from the opportunity to be raised by non-related and loving parents. In Britain alone, it is estimated that several hundred thousand people have been adopted.

Over the years there have been a small number of excellent books which have looked at adoption from the participants' point of view. Writers have asked children, adopters and birth mothers to "tell their story". This present book is in that tradition and as far as adoptive parents

are concerned, it follows in the wake of such useful contributions as Judy Austin's *Adoption: The inside story*[3] and Jerome Smith and Franklin Miroff's *You're Our Child: The adoption experience*.[4]

The present picture, though, is taken with the ever more complex demands made on adopters much more to the fore. Indeed, one of the major reasons for seeking the adopter's view was to try and recover the part which the adoptive parents themselves were playing in this busy and changing world of adoption policy and practice. Their voice is in danger of being lost and yet they remain utterly central to the success or otherwise of adoption.

Within the two main shifts of adoption philosophy, there is the danger that adopters are not seen as central characters. In extreme cases, it seems as if they have become marginal players in the adoption act. The prime shift has been away from meeting the needs of the adopters to meeting the needs of the child. In general terms this philosophy is fine but it trips lightly over some rather deep questions about the nature of child development, the quality of parenting and the significance of social relationships in family life. To ignore the needs of parents, in a sense, is to ignore the needs of children.

Also derived from the child-centred philosophy were two other developments. The first argued that children should be placed with same race adopters if the full range of children's developmental needs, including identity formation, were to be met. This left thousands of white parents and their black children feeling either guilty, confused, angry, deviant or devalued. Ironically, the needs of these parents and their children were not sensitively considered as early attacks were mounted on transracial placements. The second, as we have learnt, rethought the role and place of birth parents in the unfolding of the adoption process. More open adoptions and contact with birth parents in some form or another were advocated on behalf of adopted children and their healthy psychological development. Again, the needs of the child, as identified by adoption professionals, took precedence over the views and feelings of adoptive parents. Such practices once more sidestepped some awkward but intriguing questions about the nature of parent–child relationships, the quality of parenting, and children's social and emotional development.

Perhaps the most significant shift has been in the huge increase in the placement of older children whose psychological development has been disturbed or damaged. "Older" can mean anything from eight or nine months to adolescence in terms of the child's age at placement. But although this covers a wide range, the term "older" recognises that once children have left babyhood, they begin to accumulate a history of experiences and relationships that are likely to have an increasingly significant impact on their development prior to joining their new, adoptive family. The great needs of these children make considerable demands on parents. Most of these children are not easy to parent. And I think it is fair to suggest that many adoption professionals underestimated, and continue to underestimate, the huge impact many of these more difficult children have on adopters and their families. With the focus clearly, and even exclusively, on the needs of these unhappy and disadvantaged children, it is easy to lose sight of the needs of the adopters and any other children they might have.

Thus, on at least three counts – the emphasis on the needs of children, the arguments for more open adoptions, and the placement of older children – the role of the modern adopter has potentially become more important, more demanding and more difficult. And yet in spite of these increased expectations, and the ever more tricky emotional balancing act that adopters are being asked to perform, their views, experiences, feelings, needs, understandings and insights have been neglected. By talking to adopters and asking them to describe adoption from their point of view, this book attempts to recognise the importance and distinctiveness of adoptive parenting in these rapidly changing times.

In 1993 I set out to hear the adopter's story. I wanted parents to tell me about their experiences of adoption *from their point of view and whenever possible, in their words*. I was particularly interested to talk with parents whose children had grown up and reached late adolescence and early adulthood. Their accounts would give a personal perspective on how things had worked out in the long run. Such a view would include their experiences as adopters as well as an insider's description of the growth of adopted children into adulthood. This book, therefore, is as much about the development of adopted children – again as seen by their mothers and fathers – as it is about being an adoptive parent.

Over a two year period, beginning in 1993, I talked with the parents of 120 adoptive families. In all but one case the adoptive mother was present and she was the major informant, particularly concerning matters affecting the child in the early years. Although adoptive fathers were present in well over half the cases and their views are heard throughout these pages, there is no doubting that the voice of adoptive mothers is particularly clear and strong.

Between them, the parents had adopted over three hundred children, the majority of whom, at the time of the interview, were over the age of sixteen with many, in fact, being in their mid-to-late twenties. The parents all volunteered to help. I interviewed the parents of 120 families (91 joint interviews with both parents, 28 interviews with the adoptive mother only, and one interview with the adoptive father only). They had heard of my project through adverts in local papers, adoption newsletters mentioning my work, letters from post-adoption agencies, and by word-of-mouth from other adopters who had already been interviewed by me (this last technique, which produced the bulk of the volunteers, is known as "snowballing"). For each adopted child of the right age, the interviews typically would last between one and two hours. In several cases when parents had adopted five, six or more children I spent the best part of a day with the adopters who were not only kind enough to talk to me at great length but provided lunch as well! The talks were guided by the chronology of the adopters' experience so that we started with questions about what first made them think about adoption, through the assessment and placement phase, and on to reports of how they saw their children's behaviour, personality and development right up to the present day. As we talked, I either took notes or in the majority of cases I audio-tape recorded our conversation.

The range, variety and composition of adoptive families was both wonderful and staggering. There were baby adoptions, toddler adoptions, and the adoption of older children. There were black African, African-Caribbean and Asian children, white children, and children of mixed racial parentage. All but two children were placed with white families, although I did manage to talk with two families who had same race placements in which the adopters and children were Asian. Throughout the book, when the ethnicity of the child is not mentioned, it can be assumed that both the adopters and their children are white British. When the minority ethnic background of the child is described but not that of the adopters, these are cases in which the adopters are white and the placement is therefore transracial. The two examples of non-white same race placement are identified in the text. A few children had physical disabilities, learning difficulties or both. Some children were placed with their blood brothers and sisters.

There were parents who had not given birth to children themselves whose children were all adopted, parents who had birth children and then adopted, and parents who adopted and then had birth children. Some people adopted only one child while others adopted seven, eight, and even nine children – albeit over a twenty year period! And there were adopters who were single, married, partnered, widowed, separated, divorced or remarried (at the time of the interview). The majority of adopters might have described themselves as middle class, professional or skilled working class, with the jobs of mothers and fathers ranging from schoolteacher to priest, retired company director to practising doctor, nurse to engineer.

Because I was interested in the long-term view of adoption, the majority of parents with whom I spoke had adopted their children in the 1960s and 1970s. And as it was also my intention to let adopters tell the tale from their point of view, I was keen to use their words whenever possible. So, although I am responsible for the organisation of the material, the views expressed and experiences described are entirely those of the parents. I emphasise the dimensions of both history and the adopters' personal experience to remind readers that adoption has continued to evolve and what happened yesterday is not necessarily what happens today. Nevertheless, the voice of experienced adopters whose children are now young adults should be of great interest to other adopters, would-be adopters, child care professionals and all those who wish to further their understanding of family life and personal relationships.

To help me tell the adopters' stories, I have developed four chapters based on parents' descriptions and understanding of their children's behaviour, relationship style, personality and overall development: the secure, the anxious-to-please, the angry, and the wary and uninvolved. Otherwise, I have approached the stories chronologically. Parents talk about why they chose to adopt, their experiences of being assessed, their children's arrival and how they grew, their feelings about the birth parents, whether genes have more of an influence than upbringing, and their thoughts and reflections as they look back at the adoption of a particular child.

We begin, then, with why some people decided to adopt in the first place. In order to preserve anonymity, all names and other distinguishing details have been changed.

References

1. Rutter M, and Rutter M, *Developing Minds: Challenge and continuity across the life span*, Penguin, 1993.

2. Brodzinsky D, 'Adjustment to adoption: a psychosocial perspective', *Clinical Psychological Review*, Vol 7, pp. 25–47, 1987, USA.

3. Austin J, *Adoption: The inside story*, Barn Owl Books, 1985.

4. Smith J, and Miroff F, *You're Our Child: The adoption experience*, Madison Books, 1987, USA.

2   Wanting to adopt

For most people, the desire to have children taps into feelings which are powerful, instinctive and deep-rooted. And so having children by adoption, at first sight, seems a likely thing for people to do if they are unable to have children of their own. For many infertile couples, this is indeed the solution. However, within this simple formula, we meet a huge range and variety of motives, each coloured by normal but nevertheless quite primitive feelings to do with parenthood, fertility and reproduction. The need for children blurs with the love of children; worries about being pregnant and giving birth get mixed up with concerns about the world's population, the fragility of the environment, and the smallness of the planet. The reasons for wanting to adopt convey an idiosyncratic mixture of the personal and the universal, the unique as well as the general.

Motivations therefore vary from the desire of infertile people to have children, the wish of experienced parents to care for children in need, and the preference by some individuals and couples to form or extend their family by adoption rather than give birth to children and thereby add to the world's population problems. These categories are neither exhaustive nor mutually exclusive. Indeed, the complex nature of most people's motives meant that often it was not easy to give simple, straightforward reasons for wanting to adopt. Consequently, although it was reasonable that adoption agencies should want to explore and understand people's motivations, this was by no means an easy task. This is a book about adopters' views and so the next two chapters reflect *their* explanations, perceptions and experiences of the early stages of becoming an adoptive parent.

Infertility
Not being able to have children or not being able to have the size of family intended is experienced as a major loss by large numbers of couples and would-be-parents. Although estimates vary, the figure most

commonly quoted is one in ten couples who want children are unable to conceive. For many, it is hard to adjust to this loss. There is sadness. Often, too, there is anger as well as profound disappointment. And while people try, step by step, to cope with such feelings, at the same time they find their hopes rising and falling as doctors carry out prolonged, elaborate, and in most cases unsuccessful infertility treatments.

Infertility can affect a person or a couple and their relationship in one of four ways. First, there are those who know, even before they seriously think about having babies or meet someone, that they will never be able to have children. An accident or a childhood illness may have left them infertile. Second, there are men and women who try to have children and then discover, usually after several years without success, that this is unlikely to happen. It is at this stage that adoption is seriously considered. Third, there are parents who have adopted one or more children in the firm belief, confirmed by medical diagnosis, that they are infertile only to find, to their complete surprise and delight, that they have produced a baby. And fourth, some people, having got pregnant and given birth, then discover that they are unable to have any more children – they suffer some form of "secondary infertility". The only way they can have more children is by adoption.

Stressful times

Infertility treatment, which for adoptive parents had almost always, by definition, been unsuccessful, was rarely reported as a comfortable or pleasant experience. It was remembered by most as a stressful time which had put pressure on relationships and dashed hopes. Although in one or two instances both couples were infertile, it was more usual for one partner to be unable to have children. This could produce an imbalance as well as a strain in the relationship. 'We had tests,' stated Hester, 'and we discovered that it was my husband who was at fault. That's the only reason why we adopted.' Remmie said: 'My husband had a child by a previous marriage but I discovered I couldn't have babies. It was very hard. And on top of which I had a horrendous series of medical procedures involving operations, taking temperatures and collecting my urine. But because I felt it was more my fault, I suppose I felt I had to keep going.'

Some people needed to get their infertility out into the open before they allowed a relationship to develop. Sheila knew that she could not have children even before she met her husband: 'So I let him know just in case he wanted children and he wanted to finish it there and then. This meant we could talk about adoption even before we got married.' But even so, the days of seemingly endless treatments were remembered as distressing times.

Men with low sperm counts might blame themselves. Women who were infertile might feel guilty. The constant round of tests often put a great deal of stress on even the most solid of relationships. The medical investigations were 'hated'; the tests and procedures were 'horrific'. Mary recalls 'Time schedules, thermometers and all that kind of thing. I might have pursued it, but my husband got fed up with it all and finally he didn't want to know about it anymore.' Memories of the infertility testing sometimes bordered on the farcical for Rachel and Terry: 'Dashing across London carrying a little jar of sperm wrapped in a blanket to keep it warm! Can you imagine. It wasn't much fun and didn't do much for your sex life.'

And sometimes the behaviour of professionals did not help. Pauline and Karl had been trying for a family for several years: 'It was harrowing; terrible!' said Pauline. 'We were shunted between hospitals. An awful experience. Like at one hospital clinic, I turned up and the nurse shouted across a busy waiting room "What are you doing here today, Mrs Reid? It's not 'infertility' today."'

The irony of infertility treatment ruining people's sex life was rarely lost on couples. Partners had to make love at fixed times of the month and then rush to the hospital for some procedure. Men had to produce semen under "clinical conditions". 'We got fed up watching the calendar,' said Liz. 'If you let the medical side of things begin to rule your life, you'll never go to bed again. It has a diabolical effect on your sex life. You pay a heavy price for that. It's a little short of miraculous that we're still together.'

And while all this was going on, it seemed that the would-be parents were surrounded by a sea of babies, each one a painful reminder of their own infertility. Other people, including friends, seemed to be 'breeding like rabbits' and 'conceiving at the drop of a hat'. It 'just did not seem fair'. 'That was a traumatic time for me,' said Linda. 'I couldn't bear to pass a baby in a pram. I was getting it totally out of proportion. I got very upset.' Alma too felt devastated when she learned she could not have children. 'I became depressed and felt this dreadful emptiness. Just the two of us and this great emptiness and I'd see other people with children and that used to hurt me terribly.'

Rosemary, who was by no means unusual, admitted that she still experienced such feelings today:

'I felt vulnerable then and if I'm honest I still feel vulnerable today. If there is a film or anything which happens to involve babies being born or whatever, I always think "I missed out on that". We still don't watch, do we John? It's silly, but there was something on the other night to do with babies, and I had to switch it off . . . you know, anything to do with a woman being pregnant or birth or something and I have to turn it off.'

The reminders also came more directly from family and friends. If the infertility was still under investigation or had not been discussed outside of the couple's own relationship, strategies had to be invented and identities deployed in order to manage the information. Women at work tried to cultivate the impression that they were 'not the slightest bit interested in having children.' People's own parents could offer support and understanding one minute only to make matters worse the next: 'My younger sister got pregnant and my mother said "I'm so excited. I've never had a daughter pregnant before." I felt really put in my place.'

Enough is enough

After years of treatment, and hopes being repeatedly dashed, it came as something of a relief for many couples to be told that further medical interventions would be of no help. 'We were strung along for years,' said Pam, 'and told to go away and keep trying. But nothing happened. From the time someone finally said "You are extremely unlikely ever to have children" funnily enough it made it a lot easier. It would have been good if someone had said that a lot earlier.' Miriam shared that feeling: 'After a series of very insensitive doctors, charting my ovulations, and getting sperm counts, I began to feel incredibly inadequate and increasingly resentful. Every month I waited to see if I had a period. Anyway, once the gynaecologist suggested adoption it was actually a tremendous relief.'

However, in most cases, it was the couples themselves who decided to stop the tests and the treatments. Shirley and Richard persevered for years before they finally gave up. Shirley said, 'I did have a baby but it was stillborn. We then had seven years of infertility treatment. It was a very fraught time; very, very frustrating.' 'And because I worked in a bank and was young,' continued Richard, 'I was moved every two or three years. And so every time we went to a new area, we had to go to a new hospital and start all over again with a new specialist and a new process. In the end it got so frustrating, we said "Enough! No more!" After years of drugs, taking temperatures and watching the dates, we were worn out. Looking back though, having adopted, it was the best thing that could have happened in a way because otherwise we wouldn't have had Christopher.'

Time running out
Although the age at which people felt they were too old to be producing children of their own varied enormously, the feeling that time was running out affected a number of adopters: 'I was thirty five and time was running out. We'd had several years of infertility treatment, and nothing had happened. We wanted a family and so we went for adoption.'

A variation on this theme was less to do with being too old to have children and more about the unlikelihood of finding a suitable partner, or indeed wanting to get married, and yet still wishing to have children. Most single parent adopters described a desire to have children without either the wish or the opportunity to get married. 'I love children; I enjoy children,' said Nasima, 'but I'm not married and in my culture it would not have been appropriate to conceive a child outside marriage.' At twenty nine, Bridget realised that she 'probably wasn't going to marry'. She liked children and worked with them professionally. 'I had a comfortable home and so I saw no reason why I couldn't share my home with a child.'

However, even though it seemed that adoption was the obvious answer to the single person's problem of wanting children, many adoption agencies were not so easily convinced. Margaret 'had a very strong desire to have a family' but life had contrived to make this difficult:

'I had lost my father in my early twenties. I nursed my mother with terminal cancer up to thirty seven. I was an only daughter. I felt I had lots of home-making capacity, if you like, and having worked a great deal with children, I very much wanted a family of my own. I was forty five when my daughter was placed. I had to wait nearly five years for her! I really had to fight to gain approval. There were lots of leading questions about why I, as a single person, wanted to adopt, why I was not married, etcetera etcetera. I had a friend who had already managed to adopt as a single parent and she was a great encouragement and support. I tried to remain unruffled whatever they threw at me!'

A double loss

A few adoptive mothers had been unlucky enough to suffer two types of loss, losses which were perceived as not only ironic but also as peculiarly painful. The more common experience was to become pregnant and then lose the baby, either involuntarily through miscarriage or voluntarily by abortion, only then to discover that when it came to having another baby, secondary infertility had set in. More rarely, but with even greater heartache, were those mothers who had given birth and under social or economic pressure had chosen to have the child adopted. This is how Claire described her difficult experiences:

'When I was eighteen I got pregnant and had a child of my own. I was unmarried. My family were supportive but I decided that adoption was the best thing. And everyone said, "Well, yes, maybe it was the best thing – you can always have lots more." And of course there were no more. At the time I felt very bitter. There were not many days would go by in which I wouldn't think about Emma, my child. I could be a grandmother now. It's a weird feeling. You think to yourself "Is she alive? Is she happy? Is she a drug addict? Is she a teacher?" You swing. You imagine her as successful and lovely and then next you see on TV someone has been murdered or been in a horrific traffic accident and you just wonder, "Is that her?"'

'I then had a marriage that went drastically wrong. He had an affair and *he* had a child which brought our childless marriage to a rapid end. I remarried. We tried infertility treatment. And after tubal surgery I'd had enough and I said "No more." It was very stressful. After each procedure you think to yourself "Well, maybe this time" and you get a reminder every month when you get a period that it's not worked. When I gave up, I knew I just couldn't live by a calendar anymore. I could not have my sex life run by a calendar. I thought, "My marriage is going to go out the window here." I'd had enough. So we started talking about adoption.'

Loving and liking children

Whatever the adopters' motives, a love of children generally ran as an implicit thread through their explanations. However, a great fondness for children was the explicit and over-riding motive of a number of adopters. 'Why adopt? Well, I absolutely adore children. Full stop!' was how Beryl put it. 'The more the merrier' seemed to be the philosophy of these parents, and often they would adopt having already given birth to several children. Needless to say, in the majority of cases, they would be adopting older children, but nevertheless families of quite large size could be produced through a mix of birth, fostering and adoption spread over many years. Like mother, like daughter featured in Rita's account as she described how 'Mum always had lots of children in the house what with us and my adopted brothers and sisters as well as those she fostered and so it was all part of my upbringing. I love children. I can't really see my life without children.' Rita then went on to mention her three home-births, three adopted children, the playgroup she ran and that she was the Brown Owl for the local brownie pack.

There were also those who, although they liked children, were less keen on getting pregnant and giving birth. Caroline fell into this category: 'I know it sounds silly, but I always wanted to adopt. I just love children, but I don't like producing them! I did have two children before we adopted, but I hated the pregnancy and labour and all that bit – absolutely awful! But I simply love children. So I would have adopted all of them if I could.'

It was rare, though, for adopters to set out and plan a large family simply by adoption. Most of them said, 'It just seemed to happen by accident – first one came along and then another and before we knew it we had nine children on our hands.' Fostering was one way that children kept coming. Children who had been placed initially on a fostering basis would, after several years, become an integral part of family life. If there was no prospect or desire of returning the child to his or her biological family, then the foster child could well become an adopted child, usually to everyone's joy and satisfaction.

A final group of parents had never really thought about adoption until they were swayed or won over by an advert asking people to think about adopting an older child. If the advert had an appealing picture of the child, this would often clinch the decision to find out more. Ben and Delia saw such an advert in their local paper. They already had three children and had not really been contemplating adding to their family. But when they saw the picture, 'everything seemed to click'. For them, the idea suddenly seemed just right. 'There were these two little faces popping up in the paper,' said Ben, 'with well-written profiles telling us about them and we took it hook, line and sinker!'

Overcrowding and the world's population

Concern about the planet's ever-growing population and the pressure this puts on the environment and the quality of life was given as a reason for adopting by a number of parents. Such worries, when combined with infertility, meant that for those who wanted children, adoption was the automatic option. Even before Linda met her husband, Les, she had decided to adopt: 'Why bring any more children into the world when so many need adopting?' So when she met Les, who eventually told her that he was sterile as a result of an accident, Linda said that it was not a problem. Her reaction came as a relief to Les:

'It was as easy as that. No discussion. I was twenty two and I'd already had a broken engagement because of what had happened to me, so when I met Linda I had to tell her I couldn't have children to know how I stood. And she just said "That's all right; I've always wanted to adopt." I didn't want to go through a rejection again. That's why I told her.'

Some people chose not to have any children biologically, so concerned were they about the damage being caused by the increasing number of people in the world. This motive did not easily satisfy or convince some adoption agencies and prospective parents found that they had a lot of explaining to do.

Sue and Tim described their experiences: 'We both felt there was a choice about the way you have children,' said Sue. 'Both of us, a long time before we met each other, had decided that we actually wanted to have children, but by adoption.' Tim said:

'We were viewed by agencies as an odd couple. The first agency eventually turned us down after a long and laborious procedure. I don't think they were taking us very seriously. But when we tried another agency, they were much more willing to take our point of view and explore it with us. We were seen as odd because we'd decided not to have children the natural way. As far as we are aware, there's no medical reason why we shouldn't have children ourselves. We felt that there are too many children in the world and they too need a home. And also, more generally, there are a lot of people in the world – full stop. There is over-population. And neither of us had any particular urge to reproduce ourselves.'

Others limited themselves to one or two birth children and then chose to adopt. 'It was about twenty years ago,' recalled Steven, 'when everyone was very conscious of the world's population and we felt guilty about having another child.' Such couples accepted that their fertility would probably preclude them from being able to adopt a baby, but this did not dampen their enthusiasm.

These concerns and ethical considerations did not always go according to plan. Accidental pregnancies or the second birth child being a boy rather than the desired girl would test the strongest resolves. Ann and Martin were both clear that they wanted more than two children. Together the decision was made to have two children and then adopt. But things did not quite work out in the way intended. Ann described what happened:

'And then our plan went a little bit wrong because we had two girls and we realised that our families wouldn't really wear it if we adopted boys after girls – boys, as far as they were concerned, being more important in the scheme of things. There was a little bit of altruism in our idea to adopt. There was the sense that you can't really have more than two because the world is overcrowded as it is. But then we had the two girls and then went ahead and had a third – Matthew – who turned out to be a boy. I felt tremendous guilt when he was born because we had, in effect, given ourselves permission to have a third. But I do also remember looking at Matthew and thinking 'Good! You're a boy and so now we can adopt.'

Other kinds of altruism

As well as worries about there being too may people in the world, other adopters expressed a more direct and personal kind of altruism. The most meaningful of these were expressed by parents who had themselves been adopted. Their own experiences had been happy and it seemed that there could be no better way of saying thank you than adopting at least one child themselves.

Melissa already had three children but then decided she wanted 'to give a child a home who didn't have one'. She then added: 'I am adopted myself and so it seemed like a continuity. It worked for me. I had a good experience. I had no negative expectations, I suppose – perhaps naïvely! – I wanted to give something back in some way.' And as we shall hear in later chapters, parents who themselves were adopted felt able to understand their son or daughter in a special way which brought them closer together.

Experience and expertise

Confidence and professional skills in dealing with certain kinds of children encouraged some parents to consider adopting one or more children who had particular needs. Although Alex and Jean, who already had two birth children, felt that they could not cope with a child who had a learning disability or a child who was confined to a wheelchair, they were willing to accept a child who had a physical disability. 'Because Alex is a doctor,' said Jean, 'he knew a lot of the physical conditions we could accept and cope with. And if there were any minor problems, it wouldn't throw us.'

Iris and Graham already had an eleven-year-old daughter, Dawn, with Down's Syndrome. They had been to a lecture given by a leading expert on the condition. On the way out from the meeting hall, they noticed a little advert on a board which said that eighteen-month-old Lucille, who had Down's Syndrome and 'was a little scrap of humanity', needed a family. On their way home that night Iris said to Graham 'What do you think? Should we?' This was the first time that adoption had ever crossed their minds.

'We realised that we had something to offer. We probably could help. We'd learned something looking after Dawn. We're Christian and I have faith and I believe that they're sent for a reason – only God knows why. I mean, some people say that God only sends them to people who can cope. We had learned to cope with Dawn and we were now finding her so much easier. She had turned into a lovely girl; such a joy to have around and it seemed such a shame not to use what experience we'd got. It was a shame to waste it. All we could see was that poor little scrap who wanted a home and we could give her one.'

Finding an agency

For some people, the decision to adopt was easy compared to the difficulties encountered trying to find an agency or an agent to bring it about. Although engaging the interest and sympathies of an adoption agency turned out to be relatively straightforward and routine in many cases, in others it became a major exercise in perseverance, patience and persistence. Again, it is worth reminding ourselves that most adopters in this study were starting along the adoption road two to three decades ago. Although there was much good practice and some helpful literature, today's would-be-adopters are better served with information. For example, BAAF's book, *Adopting a Child*,[1] provides prospective parents with well-honed advice and clear signposts on where to go, how to start and what to do. But twenty or thirty years ago, parents reported a variety of experiences. Having made the decision to adopt, the next task for prospective parents was to find an adoption agency willing to consider them. This could be straightforward, but as often as not, the search for an agency could involve considerable time and effort. It could certainly demand patience.

The energy and determination required seemed to increase in proportion to some unstated measure of "differentness". If you were single or over forty, if you already had several birth children or expressed an unusual reason for wanting to adopt, if you were a short-term foster carer or from a minority religion, then two things could, but not always did follow. First, you could find it difficult to track down an agency willing to consider you. Many had only a few children available for adoption at any one time, and their "books" would be closed to new applicants. Enquirers would have to wait until the backlog had been cleared. And second, if the agency's workers were willing to consider you, they could subject you to a particularly searching assessment in order to establish your suitability.

For a large number of parents, though, the search for an agency willing to consider them was less fraught. They might have tried three or possibly four agencies, before one would eventually respond, promising to take matters a stage further. And if the enquirer was willing to consider adopting an older child or a child with some special need, their chances of receiving an encouraging reply increased even more. Of course, many parents were responding to a particular request to adopt a certain child. A child in need of a home might be advertised in the newspaper or be described in one of the specialist booklets listing children available for adoption.

After ten years of marriage and unsuccessful infertility treatment, Fred and Barbara saw a television programme which mentioned that a nine-year-old boy was looking for a home. 'We looked at each other. And I said to Fred, "What do you think? Should we have him?" So we wrote off for details and although Gary – the boy advertised – wasn't the one we eventually got, it started just like that.'

Adopting a child from overseas

People who decided to adopt a child from overseas were often prepared to go to extraordinary lengths. Vic was a soldier in the Far East. He carried out some voluntary work in an orphanage. 'The place was full of abandoned babies, particularly girls who were the result of local women getting pregnant by American GIs. Many were smuggled out of the country to places like Holland.' Vic's wife was back in England, so to all intents and purposes he was regarded as single. Vic continued his story:

'So, as a single adopter I decided to adopt a four-month-old baby girl from the orphanage. She'd been found abandoned outside the boundary fence of the orphanage left in the snow either to die or be found by the orphanage nuns. All the babies were malnourished. None of them cried because they never got a response, so they just gave up. Batch living. There was no personal care. There were hundreds of babies and toddlers in the place. Their future was grim. They'd either end on the streets begging or become child prostitutes.

'From four to eleven months I looked after Su. I cared for her during most days but she went back to the orphanage at weekends and some nights. In order to get her out of the country, I had to bribe lots of officials to speed up the paperwork. After eleven months I was moved to Singapore. I had to leave her in foster care which I had to pay for. She was a passive baby. At eighteen months she joined me as an illegal child in Singapore. Although I'd adopted her legally under her own country's law, this was not recognised in Singapore. So in Singapore, I had to be approved all over again as a potential adopter. I was visited by a social worker who asked me all kinds of questions about becoming a parent while all the time, of course, Su was sitting there listening to the questions. Bizarre! The social worker then asked: 'If you are approved, what kind of baby would you like?' And while I struggled to think how to answer such a weird question, Su was climbing on my knee! It took until Su was over two before I managed to adopt her, by which time my wife was able to join me.'

Bureaucracy, much paperwork and delay characterised most attempts to adopt a child from overseas. Patience was the greatest virtue in these circumstances. Gina and her husband were watching television programmes of the famine and the dying children in East Africa. 'We looked at each other and said "Shall we?" We went to Ethiopia almost on spec.' Not being Moslems, Gina and her husband immediately encountered problems trying to adopt any child who was suspected of being a Moslem.

'We spent a week trying to organise papers to get to the country. We eventually travelled by lorry down to Ethiopia where we visited a number of refugee camps. We met up with an American nun. She was keen to help us. There were so many starving and orphaned children. But we could only take a Christian child. So we saw hundreds of these desperate orphaned children but we were told that they were all Moslems. A month later we came home empty handed. The bureaucracy and courts were so obstructive in spite of there being hundreds of dying children. We saw some terrible sights . . .

'Six months later we returned. But again after a month, we went back empty handed. Then when we returned to England we got a letter from the American nun. She said "I know you were looking for smaller children, but there is a seven-year-old boy whose family want the boy to have a chance". After a long think, we decided yes. We then heard nothing for four months. A Sudanese lawyer helped us with the African end of things. Again, there was much paperwork. It took a year to get permission for him to leave the country! The UK Home Office was not very helpful either. My husband had to go out and sort the final details and paperwork. And finally, and after many false starts, we met Robin at Heathrow Airport! The meeting was very emotional. He was small, thin, and obviously a frightened little boy who spoke no English. Later, when he'd settled and was well integrated with our family, he told me that he was frightened because we all had blue eyes and were white. But he said he wanted to be adopted. It had always been his wish.'

And if, at the end of all this effort, whether in Britain or elsewhere, prospective parents managed to gain the interest and attention of the adoption agency, there was then the next stage in the long process of having a child by adoption – the stage of assessment. This could sometimes be even more demanding than the initial decision to adopt and the subsequent search to find a willing agency. Indeed, in many ways, and particularly in the case of babies, adopting children was experienced as a round of tests of ever increasing length and difficulty which, in the manner of Greek epics, demanded heroes and heroines whose reward for staying the course was the gift of a child. In the next chapter, we hear what adopters had to say about being "vetted" and "approved" to assume the privileged condition of parenthood.

Reference

1. Chennels P, and Hammond C, *Adopting a Child: A guide for people interested in adoption*, BAAF, 1995.

3 Perfect parents
On being assessed

Would-be-adopters accepted for consideration by an adoption agency had to be assessed to see whether or not they were suitable people to adopt another person's child. 'It seemed they were looking for perfect parents,' sighed Fran. 'We felt we had to be superhuman,' said Iona, 'if they were going to let us adopt.' The assessment process, or 'vetting' as it was often called, varied enormously in people's experience. The way adoption workers set about their task of judging people's suitability ranged from the brief and casual to the long and rigorous. More recent practices often combined assessment with preparation for adoption, although this distinction was not always appreciated by applicants. Most adopters expected to be involved in some kind of approval procedure, but views on the experience ranged from the positive and pleasant to the critical and hostile.

What unsettled some applicants was never being quite sure when they were being assessed and when they were being prepared for parenthood. It seemed safest, at least until they had their child, to assume that adoption workers were constantly weighing up their behaviour and judging it against some undisclosed standard of ideal parenting. Some parents argued that it would have been preferable to have had different professionals, ideally from different agencies, carrying out the assessment on the one hand, and providing the preparation on the other. It was easy to forget how much emotional time and energy most childless couples had already invested in trying to have a baby, even before they were assessed. Their anxiety made them feel exposed and vulnerable. In this state, they were much more alert to being scrutinised than to being prepared to take a child.

Today, adoption workers give greater emphasis to the idea of preparation rather than a simple concentration on assessment. Much time is spent on helping prospective adopters understand the kinds of children who need to be adopted. Their backgrounds, experiences and needs are considered and discussed. Implied in this approach is the question 'Given all this information, do you think adoption is for you?' Much of the preparation also takes place in groups which, along with the self-selecting quality of the preparation stage, is both supportive and empowering. Only after the stage of preparation are applicants assessed in terms of their family relationships and material stability. Much of modern-day practice, therefore, might be contrasted with parents' experiences of twenty and thirty years ago.

In those rare places where a midwife had provided specialist preparation classes for "parenthood" separate from the assessment process of the adoption agency, her independence was very much appreciated. Anita felt that 'it was good knowing that there was somebody there that you could talk to who was not actually connected with the adoption agency; someone who you know if you said something to wouldn't get back to them and spoil your chances.' Karen agreed: 'You can't open up your heart to your adoption worker and say "Look, I'm frightened about doing this" or "I don't think I could do this" because if you say anything like that you think "Oh God, she'll think I'm not capable of looking after the baby!" So you don't relate problems like that to her even though she was a warm, smashing person.'

Clearly adoption workers had to examine people's motives and suitability. The public would hardly tolerate assessment practices which were superficial and perfunctory. But to be on the receiving end of such formal enquiries was not always easy. No-one who presented themselves to an agency believed that they would not make the very best of parents. It therefore seemed both presumptuous and vaguely insulting to be assessed for parenthood. And yet all the power, it seemed, lay with the adoption worker. It was not surprising, therefore, that the whole of the assessment process was viewed with some ambivalence by the majority of parents.

Because it was such an anxious time for many, with so much resting on the outcome, various psychological strategies were adopted in the face of the investigation. These ranged from being allegedly relaxed and indifferent to feeling anxious and well-guarded against close and personal scrutiny. If the couple had already been subjected to the indignities, intrusions and ultimate disappointment of infertility investigations, they reacted in one of two ways. Either they felt well prepared for the further invasions of a psychological assessment, or they felt even more exposed and vulnerable at the prospect of yet another procedure which had to be endured on the long, uncertain road to parenthood.

Adoption workers therefore had to achieve a difficult balance between intruding further into people's already well-explored lives on the one hand and displaying care and sensitivity on the other. Sometimes workers would get the balance wrong, and sometimes the sensitivities of the parents were so near to the surface that there was no way that they could experience the "vetting" process as anything other than unpleasant, no matter how competent the assessor.

We start with those who found the assessment stage to be both useful and positive. We then hear from parents who were less happy about the "vetting" procedure.

Assessment as a positive experience

If the adoption worker was perceived as sympathetic and understanding and if the assessment process involved the transmission of information that was found to be helpful, then parents were likely to view the experience in a positive light. Everyone recognised that their suitability and aptitude for parenthood had to be examined, but the manner of that examination mattered just as much. 'We had a mixture of personal interviews at home and group meetings. They were helpful,' said Geraldine, 'and I found the woman who interviewed us very nice and understanding.' Petra already had birth children and she wanted to adopt an older child. She was keen to involve her boys in the process and so was very pleased when the agency worker said that she was more than happy to include them in the discussions. 'We had a brilliant social worker who assessed us all! Not only were the boys involved, we got support from the whole village!'

Although in many cases it seemed that the longer and more thorough the assessment, the less likely it would be that the parents would view the experience positively, there were exceptions. Eric said that their assessment was 'very intense, very serious' but in fact he found it 'quite interesting and not at all unpleasant.' But generally the rule seemed to be: the shorter the better. Sandra recalled 'only minimal vetting. Quite pleasant and rather low key. It was all very relaxed and acceptable really.'

Playing games and being defensive

Those who saw themselves as well-seasoned, realistic and even cynical, recognised that a game, as they saw it, was being played and were quite prepared to play if it meant that a child would arrive at the end of the exercise. They expressed no great belief in the value of the game. Brenda, who had undergone many years of infertility treatment, felt inured to any further invasions, whether physical or psychological:

'We had the groups and the home visits. They wanted to know all about us. We expected it. We didn't mind. Having had all the medical tests, I think you become pretty hardened. You build up a barrier. You know how much it can hurt from the hospital when one day they say "No, that's it. You won't be able to have your own." So when you come to this sort of scrutiny, you know what's expected, you say what they want to hear, and it all seems quite easy.'

In spite of knowing that she had to 'jump through the hoops', Eileen could still do little to prevent the feeling of intrusion her social worker occasioned:

'This adoption worker more or less came and camped in our house. We did offer that if he wanted to speed things up he could come and live with us. He was *so* boring! He went doggedly through his pages and pages of questions and of course he never asked us any of the important things. We had to play these boring games with him and we simply toed the line. I suppose I was both cynical and bored.'

Meg and Ray knew that there was a kind of a game being played but were not sure how to play. The nun who was their social worker also seemed nervous.

'We felt on trial all the time. She then said that her agency turned down anyone who said "No" to meeting the birth mother. She asked us what did we think. So naturally we said "Oh yes. A good idea. We'd love to meet her." She made lots of visits. It was a terribly tense time.'

Ray added: 'We were never sure what the rules were. We were told that we had to be special people, but we were never sure what the specialness was supposed to be about. The vetting took nine months altogether. It was an anxious time, I can tell you.'

Undemanding assessments

There were surprises. Expecting a thorough exploration of self and marriage, it came as something of a pleasant shock to Sarah and her husband when the assessment was carried out quickly and in no great depth. She believed that the cursory treatment was because they were both health professionals. 'It was all ridiculously easy. My husband was a medic and I was in the health service. We hardly had an interview. They took one look at us and said "That's fine" and we were put on their list.' For Penny, the assessment was 'casual beyond belief. It was a very posh adoption agency. We were both middle class, university educated and so as far as they were concerned we must be OK. It was a very snobbish agency. It all seemed dabbling sort of stuff on their part.' It seemed that a number of the "vettings" carried out in the 1950s and 1960s were of a similar perfunctory nature. If you were middle class or well connected, the approval was almost guaranteed according to some adopters. Morag said her assessment was 'undemanding.' The assessor 'was a social worker of the old school. She came to the house and said "Ah! Books . . . Ah! Pictures . . ." and we were almost home and dry.'

In one or two cases, a prolonged or searching assessment simply would not have been acceptable to the applicant. Efforts therefore were made to find an agency which would not make too many demands on the prospective adopters. Madeleine approached a small private agency in 1959. She refused to be seen by the social workers of Leeds Corporation.

'One home visit by the lady from the agency. It was very nicely done. She came to our home. It was done on a very equal footing. It was not a case of sitting on the other side of a desk and being grilled. I would have just walked out if it had. I really cannot remember any probing questions, which was important. You must remember that would-be adopters are very anxious. So she handled it all very well and didn't pry.'

Prolonged, intrusive and insensitive assessments

In contrast to Madeleine's brief encounter, other people described assessments which they found to be long, drawn out and *protracted*. Although Jan appreciated that they had to be "thorough" she was aghast at the "long-windedness" of it all: 'It took longer to be assessed than to have a baby!' All Kevin could remember was 'some young social worker who kept going on about "my feelings". "How do you feel about adoption?" she would ask. And I'd reply "OK". Then she would say "No. No. How do you *feel*?" She wanted these damn feelings all the time and I'm a down-to-earth sort of person and she just didn't seem able to cope with a straight answer. We nearly got turned down because of all these feelings.'

Many people said how vulnerable they felt. Maureen and Derek found the assessment difficult but understood its purpose. 'We had to go through all kinds of procedures,' declared Derek. 'It was a most unpleasant experience. The idea of talking about oneself for hours upon end was appalling.' 'True,' added Maureen, 'but I suppose they have to be thorough. Social services have a terrific responsibility of ensuring that they entrust young lives to safe hands.'

As well as being insensitive, some adoption workers were accused of being inflexible. Andrew and Emma already had children but were keen to adopt as well. They expected to adopt a slightly older or a mixed race child:

'The adoption worker came along with a questionnaire, a procedure that was clearly designed for childless couples. She did not gain our respect because it was perfectly clear that she could not adjust her own procedures to the fact that we were anything but a childless couple. It was formulaic. Yes, she was assessing us, but it was very superficial. Three hours all told! She never smiled. She was like a sponge. She never gave any reaction or feedback or indication of how we'd done, how long it would take, or when we would hear. She just went and left us hanging there.' 'So, we didn't go out of our way to be honest,' admitted Emma. 'We simply answered each question in a straightforward way that we knew would keep us on the straight and narrow. But what she didn't ask, she didn't get told.'

Choosing and matching

The practice of "matching" children to their adoptive parents has gone in and out of fashion, often depending on the number of babies available for adoption. The most common form of matching was to choose adoptive parents who had some physical (and sometimes social) characteristics that were similar to those of the birth mother (rarely the birth father) in the expectation that the child would blend naturally into his or her new family. If a child was matched and turned out 'to look just like dad' or 'to have our family's colour of hair', the success of the matching was viewed with satisfaction and pleasure. It often helped and never hindered the experience of adopting and being adopted. But with few babies available it is rarely practised today. When there was choice and discretion, it tended to appear in the applicant's preference for a girl or a boy, a toddler or an older child, a black child or a child with a disability. If it was not to be a baby adoption, most parents expressed some preference and this was usually met with sympathy by most adoption agencies.

Adoption workers, even with parents who had not expressed a preference, would sometimes assume that not any child would do for a couple. Ruth said:

> 'Although I always had a yen for four boys, I didn't actually mind whether it was a girl or a boy when it came down to it. But then we got this letter from the agency – full of things that we cannot show Andrea even today. I've got it here. Let me read you an example: "Although her background (Andrea's) is not as good as your own son's . . ." Can you imagine! And "she comes from a family of chefs". Chefs! And here's another one: "If you would rather wait for a baby of higher degree, do not hesitate to say so"!'

In general, single people seemed to have had a more difficult time being accepted. And as many needed to carry on working, the added requirement of only being able to take a child of school age further reduced the willingness of agencies to assess them. Neelam was a single parent adopter. It took her many years to find an agency prepared to consider her. 'I was getting subtle messages – in fact some very clear messages – that what they were looking for were "normal" families, with two happy parents.' After rejections from well over a dozen agencies, Neelam found a voluntary organisation willing to take her on. By the mid-eighties 'there was a move to ethnically sensitive matching and so after years of them saying no, I was suddenly of interest. The agency who finally took me on was very good. I was a single parent. I needed to work. And so they were quite happy to agree with my wish to have a girl of school age.'

Odd stipulations and strange requirements
Most adopters expected an assessment which would explore their views about bringing up children and would consider their established or likely parenting skills. However, in a few cases, it seemed to the parents that extra stipulations, often of an odd nature, were being built into present and future arrangements. Sometimes these amused parents, sometimes they puzzled them and occasionally they would be downright annoyed.

Margarite's assessment, carried out in the early 1960s, had gone well, though there had been worries about whether her childhood cancer had fully cleared. As a precaution the agency stipulated 'that we had to have a garden and that we had to have relatives so that the children could grow up in a normal family with cousins and aunts.'

Unhappy experiences at the hands of official agencies could drive couples to pursue a "third party adoption". Such adoptions were private arrangements, often facilitated by a third party, in which a relinquishing birth mother placed her baby directly with the adopters who only then informed the authorities that an adoption was to take place. Since the implementation in 1982 of the relevant part of the Children Act 1975 such private arrangements are no longer legal. Doris and Arthur were not impressed with the attitude of the agencies with which they had become involved:

'We tried a couple of agencies. I went to a Church one and they inter-viewed us. Being truthful, we're not church goers. So I told the man straight: "Well fair enough, if you want, I'll go to church for a year or two and when the little child is legally ours, you won't see us at church anymore." You know, I told the man this. Well, he wasn't happy with me being truthful. Then we approached another one who wanted to know if we had a bank account and this, that and the other. And I said to Arthur, "This just isn't on, you know. They're more interested in money than a child's wellbeing." That put me off. To me, to love a child, you don't need money. So I heard of this fifteen-year-old girl who'd got herself in trouble. And we did a third party adoption with her and that's how we got our Michael.'

Alice, mother of three birth children and nine adopted children, twice found herself at odds with adoption workers' ideas about who and how many she could adopt. Rachel was fostered as a toddler at first. Alice and her husband then asked to adopt the little girl. At this point, Alice became pregnant with her third child and the adoption worker told them that they couldn't adopt Rachel 'on the grounds that if I had a little girl of my own, I wouldn't want Rachel any more, which is the most stupid reasoning I've ever heard. It took us two years before we could finally adopt Rachel.' And when Alice already had five adopted children and wanted to have a sixth, her local church-based agency told her that she had enough children already. 'So me and my husband, who is a priest by the way, said "Go to blazes Church Society!" and we promptly went off to one of the Birmingham Boroughs and adopted Olivia.'

Approved and ready to go

For some the approval process was brief, pleasant and helpful. From the time of first enquiry, no more than three or four months had elapsed. For others the wish to adopt turned out to be a long, often arduous business, demanding patience and perseverance of a high order. Once approval had been granted, the speed of arrival varied from weeks to years. The lucky ones enjoyed a relatively smooth assessment, a useful induction, and the placement of their first child well within a year of approval. Those less fortunate experienced delays, set-backs and difficulties at every stage from finding an agency willing to see them, through assessment procedures which were taxing and intrusive, to a wait of several years even after approval had been secured.

But in the end, everyone received their child. It is at this point that we need to remind ourselves that we are dealing with different types of children from a variety of backgrounds placed at different ages. The patterns of adoption form the subject matter of the next chapter.

4   Patterns of adoption

The characteristics of children adopted over the last few decades have become so varied, it is no longer possible, indeed if it ever was, to see adoption as an undifferentiated experience for either children or parents. So many important things can affect a child, even before he or she is placed with a new set of parents. The age of the child at placement matters. The quality of his or her pre-placement experiences count. The number of times the child has been moved before he or she finally settles has consequences.

Children placed as young babies may have gone straight from their birth mothers to their adoptive parents with barely a break in love and care. Older children, by contrast, come with a history. The older the child, the more established his or her identity. And although many children will have been neglected or even abused over the years prior to their placement, others will have had periods of love and attention broken only occasionally by episodes of upset and distress brought on by poverty or parental illness.

Although each child's development is particular and each family's experience is unique, it is possible to recognise some broad patterns in the experience of adoption. Developmental psychologists have long been aware that childhood experiences have a bearing on many aspects of a child's development. This is not to say that there are not other important things that affect a child's development. We are all born with certain kinds of temperament and these undoubtedly influence the way others respond and treat us. Some people seem naturally cheerful and outward-going. Others may be quiet and shy by nature. And yet others can be excitable and short-fused.

Children also find themselves in different kinds of "social environment". Parents may be kind and sensitive, or they may be thoughtless and neglectful. Some families may be noisy and boisterous while others find the ability to express feelings and emotions difficult. Black African,

African-Caribbean and Asian children could find themselves with white adoptive parents.

It has already been noted that most children adopted as young babies develop normally and in developmental terms receive favourable comparison with their non-adopted peers. There are a few hints that they may show a little more anxiety and uncertainty in some social situations, but for the majority of adopted children this poses no great long-term problem. However, it does remain the case that all adopted children do have an extra developmental task with which they have to cope – they have to think about and adjust to the fact they are adopted. They do have another set of parents who, for whatever reason, chose or in a few cases were required to have them adopted. The adoptive parents also have to adjust to and reflect on the meaning of this loss as it affects both them and their children.

No matter how these issues are handled, there is no getting away from the fact that being adopted is a major piece of information about oneself which has to be thought about and understood. Adopted children have to reflect on the fact they have "lost" their first set of parents. Children only really become aware of the full meaning of adoption when they become cognitively mature and for many this means adolescence. Inevitably, being adopted raises all kinds of important questions. Why did they give me up for adoption? Was there something about me that caused them to give me away? What is the nature of my relationship with my adoptive parents? To whom do I belong? Who exactly am I? With sensitive handling and with the love and support of their families, most adopted children manage to adjust to the knowledge that they are adopted. Such happy adjustments do not mean that those who are adopted might not be curious about their biological parents, but such curiosity appears to be perfectly natural and normal.

Most children find themselves in "good enough" relationships with their parents. Communications are good; love and attention are provided in generous measure. All of this allows children to develop a clear and coherent sense of self. It also provides them with a good set of psychological skills to help them learn about their own emotional make-up as well as those of other people. They begin to learn how to handle social relationships.

Children who do not enjoy relationships which offer consistent love, interest and attention find it hard to make sense of what is going on. The world of other people seems unpredictable, unreliable and uncertain. If relationships provide the experiences in which we learn about ourselves and others, children who are denied good quality relationships find it hard to develop coherent "models" which help them understand their own feelings and emotions as well as those of others. In a sense, they are less socially competent; the social world for them is a less intelligible and therefore experienced as a more difficult and puzzling place.

No matter what kind of relationship children have with their mothers and caregivers, somehow they have to survive emotionally. Children who are neglected or abused, ignored or confused have to make the best of a bad job. They have to develop ways of coping with the emotional stresses and strains of being cared for by someone who is unreliable or hostile, inconsistent or dismissive. Many of the toddlers and older children who are eventually placed for adoption will have had a history of poor quality and difficult relationships with their mothers or fathers. Such children will have developed psychological strategies to try and cope with these emotionally adverse experiences. It is these pre-established ways of trying to cope which adopted children bring with them when they join their new families. If adopted children and their behaviours are to make sense, it is important to appreciate and understand how their relationship histories influence their personalities, social behaviour and ability to handle current relationships.

I might also introduce the concept of *resilience* at this point. There is no doubting that some children, in spite of experiencing great adversity prior to their placement, managed to cope well with childhood after placement and showed little in the way of seriously disturbed behaviour. Psychologists, such as Fonagy and his colleagues,[1] identify a number of defining attributes of resilient children including easy temperament; removal from the adverse environment; absence of early separation or losses; a good, warm relationship with at least one caregiver; availability in adulthood of good social support; a positive school experience; high IQ; and a sense of humour. In the case of adopted children, this means that a few who have suffered harsh and disturbed care prior to adoption, might nevertheless make a reasonable emotional recovery and enjoy secure relationships with their new families. However, our understanding of the many ways in which resilience might be achieved is still rather limited and at the moment we have only a few basic ideas of explaining why some older placed children fare better developmentally than others.

Listening to and thinking about what adopters said about their children's relationships and behaviour, progress and achievements, I identified several very broad patterns of adoption. In many cases, a particular *post-placement* pattern of behaviour and development was associated with a child's *pre-placement* history of relationships prior to being adopted. But as we have seen in the case of resilient children, there are always exceptions even to this simple rule. In telling the adopter's story, it was possible to recognise four general patterns:

- Secure children;
- Anxious-to-please children;
- Angry children;
- Uninvolved and wary children.

Similar patterns, of course, might be found in any group of children whether adopted, fostered or not. However, one or two things *are* different for adopted children: all adopted children have two sets of parents; and older adopted children have experience of at least two families. The majority of older placed children (whose age at placement can range from eight or nine months up to adolescence) will have experienced some type of adversity prior to joining their new families. Moving from an adverse environment to a benign one, again though not unique to older-placed adopted children, is sufficiently unusual to make the story of their development interesting.

Although the stories told in this book are not compared statistically, it might be noted that African, African-Caribbean, Asian, and children with a mixed ethnic background who were placed with white British parents featured in all four categories at rates statistically similar to white children in same-race placements.[2,3] Black or 'mixed parentage'[4] children placed as babies were just as likely to be described as secure and successful by their white adoptive parents as white children placed as babies. Children from minority ethnic backgrounds and white children with adverse pre-placement histories were both equally liable to experience some developmental difficulties. Of course, the accounts given and experiences reported are those of *parents* and not those of their adopted sons and daughters. The stories and perspectives of the grown-up adopted children would be another tale, but here we concentrate on the voice of the parents. Although parents spoke with concern and sensitivity about the racism that their children experienced, the developmental impact, if any, of being transracially placed was not something about which parents felt able to express an informed psychological opinion.

Two or three of the above categories might look somewhat alarming to the reader unfamiliar with either the wide range of adoption practices or the work of child psychologists. It is worth emphasising, and it will be repeated, that the biggest category of adopted children in terms of numbers, particularly amongst those placed as babies, is that of secure children. But just as some children who remain with their birth families experience behaviour problems, a number of adopted children experience developmental difficulties and upsets. For adopted children, these difficulties may originate in:

- the child's own natural make-up and disposition;
- the quality of care and parenting he or she experienced before being adopted;
- the quality of care provided by the adoptive family;
- relationships with and feelings about brothers, sisters, peers and the wider community;
- the very condition of being adopted itself, irrespective of any of the other factors; or
- the complex interaction between any two or more of these ingredients.

There was nothing automatic about a child who had experienced disturbances and difficulties before being placed at the age of three or four becoming "angry" or "uninvolved". There were examples of children who had had a raw deal in their early years becoming well-established and reasonably secure in their new families. Both children and families were capable of showing considerable resilience in the face of adversity. But in spite of the many exceptions, it was possible to detect a general pattern in which children with the more disturbed, upset and damaging experiences prior to joining their new families showed greater anxiety and insecurity throughout their childhoods.

Very experienced and confident adopters might be able to handle and live with quite difficult children in which case outcomes were often very happy. However, some difficult children proved too much for less experienced or less confident parents and in these cases things might not turn out so well. But some children's behaviour could be too disturbed even for accomplished adopters. These parents found themselves having to "hang on in" to prove to their children that they were loved. The four patterns therefore illustrate the range and combinations of parent–child relationships as described by adopters.

But before we start exploring each of the four main groups in more detail, we need to take a look at baby adoptions from the time the baby arrived to the day the adoption was made. Historically, baby adoptions are still the most common, and it was interesting to learn how couples coped with the arrival of a baby, often after years and years of waiting.

References

1. Fonagy P, Steele M, Steele H, Higgit A, and Mayer L, 'The theory and practice of resilience', *Journal of Child Psychology and Psychiatry*, 35:2, pp 231–58, 1994.

2. Howe D, 'Adoption and attachment', *Adoption and Fostering*, 19:4, pp 7–15, BAAF, 1995.

3. Howe D, 'Parent reported problems in 211 adopted children: some risk and protective factors', *Journal of Child Psychology and Psychiatry* (forthcoming).

4. Tizard B, and Phoenix A, 'The identity of mixed parentage adolescents', *Journal of Child Psychology and Psychiatry*, 36:8, pp 1399–1410, 1995.

5 Adopting babies
From placement to adoption order

Historically, most adoptions have been baby adoptions. These reached a peak in 1968 when, in England and Wales for example, over 16,000 babies were placed with non-related parents. With changes in the social climate, contraceptive practices, abortion rates and family support, the number of babies adopted today has dropped dramatically to considerably less than a thousand a year. Nevertheless, this still means that several hundred thousand people up and down the country were adopted as babies.

Researchers have shown time and again that in the majority of cases, children adopted as young babies grow up into well-adjusted adults, barely distinguishable in most psychological respects from their non-adopted counterparts raised in similar families.[1,2] It seems, then, that baby adoptions in most cases have been a success story. There are some exceptions and these are discussed in Chapters 9 and 10.

Given their numbers and satisfactory outcomes, this ought to mean that this chapter and the next, both of which concentrate on baby adoptions, should occupy most of the book if they are to fairly represent the overall story of adopters on adoption. However, the very success of these children seemed to mean that most parents believed that there was not much to say about their sons and daughters: 'They grew up, went to school, found a job, got married and lived happily ever after' was hardly an exaggeration if most parents were to be believed. Several adopters said, by way of introduction, 'Well, there's not much to say to be honest. All a bit boring really!' What they meant was clear enough. Their stories lacked the drama, upset and incident of those whose children found growing up more difficult. Like all basically happy stories and good news, the strength of the accounts lay in the everyday ordinariness of the children's development.

Although a few babies appear to have been very disturbed and upset by their first one or two moves, most seem to have settled quickly into their new families. Some were transferred directly from birth mother to adoptive mother in one move. Others arrived in their new homes via a foster carer or a hospital ward for premature babies. In some cases, the babies were with their new mothers within a few days of birth. But more typically, the infants were placed after several weeks of being looked after by either their birth mother or a foster carer.

The patterns of development described in this chapter and the next are best described as "secure". Children experienced rewarding, reciprocal and trusting relationships with their parents. They formed strong, secure attachments with their mothers and fathers. Sound, confident and socially competent selves emerged. The children handled their adoptive status well. Transitions into adolescence and early adulthood were negotiated relatively smoothly with no more than the usual ups and downs experienced by any well-adjusted individual.

We join parents at the point back in the 1960s and 1970s when they have been approved by an adoption agency and they are waiting for their first baby. We then follow developments from the baby's arrival to the parents' first experiences of looking after an infant.

Waiting and preparing

In the case of most baby adoptions, the time between approval and placement varied from a matter of weeks to several years. Typically, though, parents found themselves waiting around nine to twelve months. During this time, most people simply tried to get on with their lives. Women carried on working, never really knowing when the telephone call would come telling them a baby was ready and waiting. They steadfastly refused to get over-involved with the thought of an infant arriving – 'just in case.' For those who had suffered the rigours of infertility treatment, they had learned not to raise their hopes. 'So as not to tempt fate,' said Morag, 'I wasn't at all prepared. So when she came at two days notice, I'd no idea what to do! Being at home with a baby suddenly made me feel trapped. I was totally responsible and there was no escape.'

But trying to give shape and structure to this period of waiting was not easy. There were none of the usual benchmarks associated with having a baby. It was like a pregnancy of unspecified length with very little warning about which day the baby would arrive. 'Like a big void,' was how Lara described it. All of which was in marked contrast to the assessment phase: 'When they were processing you, interviewing you, it was all going on . . . letters, coming to visit you, telling you this, that and the other. And then suddenly you go on their lists and you don't hear anything from them . . . You know it's going to happen but it did seem unreal.'

Although most people, particularly those who were unable to conceive children, purposefully decided to make no preparations, a few did feel the need to prepare themselves in some way. Some began to cut down their hours of work. They sought to "acclimatise" themselves to motherhood by taking a greater interest in all things to do with children and babies. Sarah did not want 'to count chickens' but she did decide to help a friend down the road who had twins. She helped bath and feed the babies. 'I thoroughly enjoyed it. It gave me some confidence.' In one or two parts of the country, locally enterprising midwives had set up preparation classes especially for childless adopters. Couples viewed these opportunities very favourably. The classes were independent of the adoption agency and did not involve pregnant women. The support of other couples was felt to be particularly important and many parents who shared the classes formed life-long friendships. The meetings, held at regular intervals, had the added bonus of giving a timescale to that period between approval and placement when they felt in "limbo".

The offer
Most people had tried to stop thinking about when the offer of a baby would be made – 'you'd go mad if you raced to the phone every time it rang.' They defended themselves against their anxieties by switching off any thoughts to do with babies. So when the call did eventually arrive, it often came as a shock and surprise. People were not prepared. Superstitions and fears of tempting fate meant that cots had not been bought, thoughts about how to feed the baby had not been made. Often there would be only two or three days between the telephone call and the baby's appearance. 'I remember the call so well, totally out-of-the-blue – "Mrs Talcot, we've got a baby boy for you. Can you come and collect him from the hospital this afternoon?" "This afternoon!" I thought. So we went there and then, and took him home. He was gorgeous.'

The result generally 'was a mad dash around Mothercare grabbing anything that seemed relevant to bringing up a baby!' Of course, many women were in jobs, so on top of everything else, they had to give in their notice, quickly wind down their work, and start thinking babies. The drama and the farce of assuming motherhood at two days notice was nicely captured by Sarah:

'I got a phone call at work, out of the blue, having completely forgotten about adoption. I remember downing tools and going straight to the administrator, saying "Right! No more work for me. I've got a child!" Tom was just four days old. I remember going into Boots wearing jeans and a tight tee-shirt looking very un-pregnant and saying "Help. I'm having a baby. What do I want?" And then in the next shop, I went to buy nappies and a rather elderly, rather condescending assistant looked at my bare tummy exposed between my tee-shirt and jeans and said "It is exciting, isn't it dear. When's it due?" as if to say "You silly girl. Why the hell are you panicking." So I said "He's due on Monday" and her faced dropped and I think the nappies too.'

Ray was ungenerous enough to think that when Meg telephoned him at work she must have crashed the car: 'I couldn't think why else she'd be phoning.' They then rushed around collecting prams, borrowing cots and buying clothes. 'And then when I couldn't get the steriliser to work,' said Meg, 'I burst into tears. It all seemed too much. I thought "Oh God, this baby is going to die of gastro-enteritis." I was so uptight.'

It was not unusual for parents to feel the enormity of what they were taking on only at the last moment. Having been approved as potentially first-rate parents, having psychologically switched off from thinking about babies because of anxieties and superstitions, and having made no preparations, the sudden arrival of a major life-change in the form of a week old baby could tax the strongest spirits. 'It was not like a pregnancy. There was no build up. We got no help. No midwife. No health visitor just when you most needed one because you were scared. It was Wednesday and we were told James would arrive on Friday. We were just expected to get on with it. I froze. It was a difficult experience for me suddenly taking this strange, dark-skinned, very beautiful little child. I just looked dazed.'

False starts

One of the most unsettling as well upsetting ways to begin one's parent-hood as an adopter was to have a baby placed with you and then for that baby to be reclaimed by his or her birth mother. Not only was this always a painful experience – 'a bloody time, an awful time' – it undermined people's confidence. It meant that anxieties were inevitably raised when the next baby arrived: '. . . it affects how you start to feel about the next baby. Can you totally commit yourself? Is there a chance they'll be taken away?' Seven weeks after placement, Jenny's baby was reclaimed by her mother. I felt absolutely devastated. When we had the next one – Henry – it was terrible. Every time there was a knock on the door I got so ner-vous and frightened. Our own older daughter kept asking when was she going to be sent away too. It made us very edgy with poor little Henry.'

Several parents compared their loss to a bereavement. But in spite of the traumas, for every false start there were at least twenty solid begin-nings.

First sight, first contact

At first sight, some babies, according to their adopters, looked ugly while others appeared "just beautiful". Some babies were delivered to the door, others were seen in hospital cots. Babies were first seen crying and yelling in the arms of a foster mother while others were handed over in person by the birth mother. But whatever the method, the occasion was always remembered in detail and often with emotion:

'The letter came from the agency and she sounded perfect. And it was such a thrill. I went with an empty carry-cot and getting a baby . . . well, it's the most incredible feeling. It makes me want to cry to describe it now. It is just the most incredible experience. Wonderful. It's such a gift. This tiny baby one is being asked to have. I saw this wonderful baby who looked up at me and started to gurgle. We took her home and it was bliss.'

'Love at first sight' was common. 'As soon as we saw her, we both knew, without even looking at each other, that we wanted her, that she had to be ours.' Chloe was ten days old when Elaine first saw her. '"Undress her. See what you think. Have a good look," ordered the adoption worker. And she was beautiful. We were over the moon.' Family similarities were often perceived, as if to confirm that this really was 'our baby.' 'He was just seven days old,' said Beattie, 'and I fell in love with him. He was beautiful. He had blue eyes and blonde hair – just like my husband!'

Speed of delivery, even a sort of peremptoriness on the part of adoption workers seemed not an infrequent experience. Sandra had been invited along to the agency office simply to discuss a possible baby, as she thought. 'And when we got there, we were shown this baby. "Do you like her?' they asked. "Err. Well. Yes," we replied. "Well, you can take her then. Off you go." That was it. Off we went home with our baby! We'd made absolutely no preparations.' Alan, Prue's first baby, was ten days old when he was "delivered" to her home. 'The old adoption worker – she must have been near retiring – drove up, marched to the gate with the baby in one arm and a tin of dried milk in the other and said "He's ready for his two o'clock feed" and left me to get on with it!'

A few parents described how, upon first seeing their son or daughter, they suddenly realised that they were about to take home with them another woman's baby. Feelings of discomfort and unease would sweep over them. Lucy first saw Rachel lying in a cot on a hospital ward:

'I felt very uncomfortable. I had no experiences of babies. I didn't know what to do. We got her home and I just burst into tears and sat down and cried and cried and cried. I thought "I cannot take this baby away from her mother. You've got to take her back. It's not my baby. I can't steal this baby." But when the baby cried that night and needed me, that helped because suddenly I had to do something. It was a very odd and difficult first day. All those years I'd longed for a baby and all I kept thinking was that she wasn't really mine.'

Richard had been a premature baby, the son of a Welsh nurse and a visiting academic from Mauritius. He had been with a foster mother for five months until his birth mother finally decided that she would relinquish him for adoption. June recalled first seeing him and how upset his mother was at the hand over:

'He was dressed in beautiful white and the foster mother said – it was all very melodramatic – "Take him! Take him!" She was crying and I felt desperately sorry for her especially as he wasn't like my own child at that point. I didn't know him. I took him home and felt very worried and scared and lonely. And he cried all that night and was very difficult no doubt thinking to his little self "Where on Earth am I and who is this woman holding me now?" He was clearly missing his foster mother.'

A particularly odd experience was described by a number of adopters who were given a choice of which child to take home. This was most likely to be true for some of those who ventured overseas to adopt their baby. They would be ushered into a noisy nursery full of babies in cots and asked to choose.

Meant to be

Those who believed that it was 'love at first sight' or that 'she looked just like my side of the family' suggest the operation of an important psychological need for the baby to be claimed and owned by the adopters; that the infant really was, in some metaphysical way, their baby. An even stronger version of this process was seen when parents first saw their baby and for whatever reason they knew that it was 'just meant to be'. This particular baby was destined to be their child. Penny and her husband had gone to visit ten week old Dominic at the mother and baby home:

'We had decided to call him Dominic. In fact, ever since we'd been approved a couple of years earlier we had been thinking of our future son as Dominic. And just as we were leaving with him to go home I turned to the Matron and asked "Oh, by the way, what's he been called?" And she said, "Oh no, you must choose. Choose whatever name you like." "Well," I said, "we've already decided to call him Dominic." "Good heavens," she said, "That's what he's been registered as already. All his clothes have got that name sewn into them." It was as if it was meant to be.'

Birthdays, too, could indicate that a baby was fated to join a family. 'Tom,' said Christine, 'was born on Harriett's birthday! It was just like he was made for us. It was really nice. And ever since, Tom and Harriett have been very close.' Roger was nine weeks old when Sheila first saw him. He was born on March 7th. 'Incredible really,' said Sheila. 'Many of my husband's family have a birthday in exactly that same week and it was tradition in our family to celebrate that week. So Roger was bound to be a Tranter! He fitted in because of his birthday.'

Meeting the birth mother

At the time when most of these adoptions took place, it was relatively rare for adopters to meet the baby's mother. But it did happen. Although most adopters were apprehensive and anxious about the meeting, looking back many were glad they had met their child's parent. They had a real person to describe; there was a tangible contact that linked the adopted child and his or her two sets of parents.

Typical in their feelings were Maeve and her husband. 'Josh was three weeks old when we saw him and his mother,' said Maeve. 'She was from Panama. We think the father was Italian. And we met her and I remember it was terribly upsetting. I felt like a kidnapper. She handed her over.' 'But looking back,' said Derek, 'we were glad it did happen like that because we can visualise her. It was a very emotional occasion for everybody. She wanted to see us and to see who she was handing her baby over to. We were all weeping.'

Such meetings allowed adopters to understand something of the birth mother's dilemma. Their feelings towards her would warm. And in later years it seemed that not only could they physically describe their son's or their daughter's mother but they could also convey something of the love and the emotion that surrounded the hand over. Eileen's second child was five weeks old when they saw him in the arms of his young Filipino mother. She already had one child, she was young, she was in England, and she felt she just could not cope with another baby:

'She wanted to meet us. I was apprehensive. We met. It was very desperate. I can't imagine how you ever make that decision. She was a lovely woman. Really nice and she had to make this hugely tough decision and you feel that life is so unfair for some people. She was convinced that she was doing the right thing by Luke. Of course, you can't go away from a meeting like that and say your joy is based on somebody else's sadness. Looking back, I'm very pleased I did meet her. I can feed in to Luke very positive images of his mother.'

Adopters who had the chance to meet the birth mother at the time of the hand over but did not take up the opportunity, reflected on their decision in contrasting ways. Madeleine, thirty years later, was still adamant that she had had no wish to meet her son's mother: 'No. I would never wish to meet her. I wouldn't want to know what she looked like. In fact, I don't want to know anything about her, except that she wasn't a tart. She was in fact a dental assistant.' But Sarah was not so sure now. The birth mother was sixteen.

'We were offered the chance to meet her but we didn't want to. I had this horrific thing that she was going to be fat and spotty although I suspect she was in fact rather pretty but I thought it might colour my opinion about what my daughter would grow up to look like. It seemed the right decision then but if you asked me today I think I probably would have wished to meet her. At the time I was feeling very insecure.'

But one mother who did meet both the birth parents, now wishes that she had not. Their image haunted Lena and she was plagued by uncomfortable feelings of guilt, even now, over twenty years later. The birth parents were two bright undergraduates. The meeting with them went well 'but looking back I wish I hadn't met them. I know so much about them. They're still together. At the time they were under parental pressure to give the baby up . . . I don't know what to do if Dan wants to start searching. I just can't get his birth parents out of my mind. I do wish I hadn't met them. I feel if Bill and I were to die, say in an accident, I would want Dan to go back to his natural parents rather than anyone else. I feel I've taken away their child. I see their family as incomplete because I've got their son. And yet I also fear they'll find him and take him away. And I worry that Dan will want to go, that he'll want to live with them.'

The first few weeks

Two things happened in the first days and weeks after the baby's arrival. One was immediate and practical – babies demanded a lot of care. The other was subtle and emotional – a relationship needed to develop between infants and their carers. For some parents a "bond", a feeling of love was there almost from the start. For others, such feelings took a little longer to become established. And for an unfortunate few, the close attachment that forms between most babies and their caregivers was never really achieved.

There was also a difference between first-time parents and old hands. Like all new parents, many found themselves checking every half hour to see whether or not their baby was still alive and breathing. The more experienced parents adopted a more relaxed attitude to the latest addition to their family. This did not necessarily mean that these babies were going to be easier to look after than their older brothers and sisters. It could come as a shock to some parents to suddenly find that just when they thought they had "cracked" how to look after babies, the second, third or fourth would turn out to be demanding, difficult and a real handful. Nevertheless, the experience did help. Parents who had successfully coped with several young children had no real doubts about their abilities as parents. So, even though the newcomer was proving to be less amenable to their skills, parents remained relaxed and confident, knowing that it was more likely to be something to do with the baby and not their competence as carers. However, this assuredness was not so readily available to first-time parents. If they had a difficult baby, there was always that nagging worry that the problem might be because they had poor parenting skills, and 'maybe they were never really meant to have children.'

Some children appeared to be naturally accomplished as social beings. Their easy-going and likeable natures stayed with them throughout their lives. Matt's mother was a young woman 'more interested in her career than becoming a single parent'. Matt joined Julia and her husband when he was five weeks old and 'he was a wonderfully straightforward baby. In fact he's been a relatively straightforward, likeable person throughout his life and he's now thirty three.' But even if a mother had a perfect baby, she may not have felt that she was the perfect mother. 'We got Callum home,' recounted Naomi, 'Our baby! And it was unbelievable bliss and unbelievable hell all at the same time. I was overwhelmed with delight at this young child and I was also terrified because it was all down to me! But he was a perfect baby.'

Like many parents, Sarah not only thought that she had 'a happy baby, a beautiful child, a dear little boy' but she also believed that she had 'an exceptionally intelligent child who was into everything, very forward, and once he got talking he soon had a terrific vocabulary.' It seemed important for many adopters to recognise some out-of-the-ordinary ability in their child – he walked at nine months, she had a reading age years ahead of her peers, he was a genius at maths, she had an IQ of over 150, he was brilliant at art.

But for all the babies who arrived content there was an equal number who started off difficult and demanding. 'He was the complete opposite to Louise,' said Eileen. 'Luke was a difficult baby – he still is in some ways! He was highly demanding. He never seemed to be satisfied and I would be up with him throughout the night and this went on for years. He now works nights as a computer trouble-shooter, would you believe!'

This feeling of having to be the perfect parent, which was the direct result of the intensity of the assessment process, initially confused and inhibited a number of mothers. Philip's birth father was an Indian lawyer and his mother was a white English secretary. He was placed with adopters at six weeks:

'It felt like running a guest house when the guest might up and go at any time. And while he lay there I was trying to convince myself that I really loved him, knowing that it was not actually true. I was so worried that I ought to be doing everything right. I felt under so much pressure that everything had to look right and be done right. That pressure squeezed out all my feelings. And then after five weeks of this I suddenly thought "I'm not going to fuss about how the house looks; I don't care of it looks a mess and I look a mess when the social worker visits." I'd come out of the freezer and given myself permission to have feelings. And from that moment on I knew I'd die for Philip. He was thoroughly mine.'

Babies who were not easy seemed to slow down the bonding process. Ian was born slightly prematurely. Lena described him as a noisy, restless baby who 'screamed night and day' and wore her out. 'There were times I just wanted to get away and it definitely slowed down my bonding with him.' Luke, too, was a difficult baby. He would not be left alone and wanted attention all the time. 'It interfered with my bonding with him,' said Eileen, 'and I felt partly guilty because

I felt I ought to be loving him. My husband stepped into the breach and he and Luke did become close.'

Babies who were difficult and cried inconsolably tended to stir up a mother's feelings of inadequacy. In contrast, babies who were unwell and appeared even more helpless and dependent made mothers feel needed. 'For the first few days I seemed to be just going through the motions with Daniel. I was being mechanical and only my sister-in-law suspected that I was worrying that I might not actually like him. But at twelve days old, he got very ill with projectile vomiting. And as soon as he got sick, poor little thing, I became utterly devoted to him. I suddenly felt protective of this helpless little creature.'

A few mothers who had already breast-fed their older children wanted to try it with their adopted baby believing that it would help the bonding process as well as provide some natural milk. The biggest problem was trying to get the milk supply going and although it was unlikely that the baby would be entirely sustained by the breast milk, most of those who tried it felt that the attempt had been helpful and worthwhile. Ben, whose birth parents were both African-Caribbean, was placed with a white family when he was three weeks old. Wendy recalls that she 'tried breast-feeding him and he got a little milk.' He was a 'scrumptious baby' and in contrast to his rather demanding older brother, he was placid and just perfect for us:

'Ben came with an air of being loved. His mother had prepared a beautiful layette for him and I thought he was absolutely beautiful. I had a go at breastfeeding him. He was getting a little milk but then I began to feel ill. My breasts were getting sore and bigger. And then I discovered I was pregnant. This was before Ben's adoption had gone through. The adoption agency were a bit huffy about my pregnancy. But by then we loved Ben so much. I told them I was prepared to have an abortion rather than lose Ben. I don't think I actually thought through what an abortion meant but you could see how earnest I was about Ben. Anyway, the adoption agency eventually relented and said "This baby is an act of God and we suppose you'll manage." And we did.'

The final ingredient which affected the attachment process, at least as far as the parents were concerned, was the tricky time between the baby's placement and the granting of the adoption order which usually took place several months later. A few took it for granted that the adoption would go through. They had no worries whatsoever.

But we have heard already that some adopters had the unhappy experience of having a baby placed with them only for the infant to be reclaimed by the birth mother. Not surprisingly, these parents remained anxious until the adoption order was finally made. In fact, Molly, whose first baby was returned to the birth mother, had a recurring dream about the twins she adopted:

'Of course I was anxious up to the adoption order with the twins. For several years after I'd have a dream in which I couldn't get to them. I'd lost them. Or they'd be going away from me and somehow I couldn't get them back. Very weird, very frightening, very distressing dreams.'

But other adopters, too, experienced various levels of anxiety and in one or two cases it seemed to inhibit the bonding process. They 'held back'; their total emotional commitment was tempered – just in case. It was a time of slight insecurity for many, though by no means all. These were people who had had years of infertility treatment in which hopes had been raised only to be dashed. They could not afford to be hurt again.

Jan had a particularly harrowing experience. Her worst fears seemed about to come true. Becky had been placed with them when she was five weeks old. Then after two months they were hit by a bombshell.

'The birth mother wanted her back. We were totally shattered. I could hardly touch Becky, I loved her so much. It was very, very painful. A week went by and then the birth mother changed her mind. I think for about a year thereafter it affected my relationship with Becky. I seemed reluctant to commit all my emotions so totally again. She tended to be a daddy's girl for this period. I was so terrified I was going to lose her again. But after a year, I was back to normal and in the end everything worked out wonderfully.'

By this time, the baby, now legally adopted, was usually well into the second half of his or her first year. Sound relationships between parents and child were established. The child's character and personality were beginning to emerge and parents had a good idea what kind of budding individual they had on their hands. Most of these adopted babies grew into confident and competent children. Other children, too, adopted at older ages settled well into their new family life. These two groups of children generally felt "secure" in their relationships with other people. The next chapter picks up their story.

References

1. Seglow J, Pringle M, and Wedge P, *Growing Up Adopted: A long-term national study of adopted children and their families*, NFER, 1972.

2. Fergusson D M, Lynskey M, and Horwood L J, 'The adolescent outcomes of adoption', *Journal of Child Psychology and Psychiatry*, 36:4, pp 597–616, 1995.

6 Secure children

In secure patterns of attachment we see relatively trouble-free, straight-forward, satisfied and satisfying childhoods. This is not to say that some children did not get into trouble at school or that some adolescents did not row with their parents, but by and large, relationships between parents and children were viewed as normal, acceptable and pleasurable. Childhood was experienced positively by both parents and children. Transitions through the various stages of growing up passed without too much upset. There was a balanced feel to parent-child relationships. The child's sense of self and emerging personality were strong. Self-esteem and confidence were basically sound. Other people were trusted and valued which helped children to feel secure in their relationships. There was little doubt in the children's minds that they were loved and wanted. These personality traits and relationship styles saw the children happily through into adulthood and independence.

Most of the children in this group had been adopted as babies, but there were certainly examples of older placed children who had experienced some upset and adversity prior to being placed with their new families. The *resilience* shown by some children remains unclear and complex. As mentioned in Chapter 4, factors ranging from natural temperament to strong support in later relationships have all been associated with a good developmental outcome for children who have suffered a poor start in life.

Within this secure pattern we find sociable children and shy children; bright children and slow children; excitable children and quiet children. All the children had an inner strength of self which allowed them to cope reasonably well with life's upsets and difficulties. Life was approached confidently and constructively. Based on parents' descriptions, four groups of secure children were recognised:

- the easy going;
- the determined, organised and optimistic;

- amblers; and
- late starters.

The easy going

These children coped with life without fuss. They were liked and well-regarded by parents, teachers and friends. They moved into adulthood fairly effortlessly. People saw them as able, competent and mature. Relationships with their parents and family remained good. They coped well with relationships in adult life, and if they had children, they became relaxed and confident parents. Most found jobs fairly readily. These children seemed to be universally liked. The words used most often to describe them included gregarious, energetic, sociable, friendly, loving and loved.

Andrea

Andrea, born slightly prematurely, was 'a gorgeous little baby and incredibly easy to look after.' According to her mother, Ruth, 'she had a lovely nature – and still has. She was a beautiful child who got on with everyone. Her brothers loved her and she loves everyone.' Andrea enjoyed school. She worked hard and had many friends. The teachers always described her as 'a delightful child'. She never lost her temper and adolescence passed by without upset. After passing her 'A' levels, Andrea went to University and achieved a modest degree in English. She now works in publishing and 'she is very happy'. Andrea, with her parents' support, thought that one day she would search for her birth mother. She had always been interested in her adoption in an open, relaxed way, wondering with Ruth what her birth mother might look like and whether she might have other brothers and sisters.

But even for the most serene children, life could throw up some odd, even cruel ironies. Matt was always loved and liked. He qualified as a doctor, then became a musician, and married in his mid-twenties. The couple then discovered they couldn't have children and decided to adopt. Up until then he had shown no interest in his own adoption. He met his own baby's birth mother and he said that this experience acted like an 'absolute trigger' to search for his own birth mother. Although the search was successful – his birth mother turned out to be a nationally prominent figure – his relationship with her was not entirely successful. The inner strength and confidence possessed by children like Matt meant that they had the emotional resources to cope with even severe upsets and problems.

The determined, organised and optimistic

Some children appeared to get a grip on life from the word go. They set about school, exams, relationships and all the challenges of growing up with a winning combination of optimism and determination. They had energy and everyone felt that their successes were thoroughly deserved. They were both liked and admired for their positive attitude.

Mandy

Mandy's first three months prior to being placed with Linda and Robert were 'chaotic'. Her mother was African-Caribbean. Mandy was 'handed around like a little parcel from mother to hospital to foster mother to me.' She was a beautiful baby but passive. 'She didn't come out of her shell until she was eight months old.' Throughout her childhood, Mandy had 'always wanted to do things correctly. She was easy to bring up. She knew when she could do something and she knew when she couldn't. She's a very organised person.'

Her schooldays were trouble free except for the ever-present racism that black children experience. 'Whereas her older brother would tell us nothing, Mandy would come home and cry and say "Why can't I be white like you mummy?" ' Over the years, Linda gave Mandy very positive views about being black. 'She is now a beautiful, poised young woman who is both pleased with and proud of herself.' Bright, sociable and with lots of friends, Mandy became the first black Head Girl of her all-girls school. 'She's very diligent and she works hard,' said Linda. And with her three good 'A' levels, Mandy went on to read History at University 'and loved every minute of it.' One day, she thinks she will search for her birth mother, 'but not yet'.

These "determined" children, though basically secure and successful, still felt that they had to try that little bit harder and were still nagged by little twinges of anxiety. Beth said of her son: 'I believe Philip's determination to achieve is partly to try and prove to the world that an adopted boy can do well.' Twenty five years later, Philip, with 'dogged determination' gained high level science degrees 'and he's done very well and we're proud of him.'

Even children who had a poor start could tackle life head-on and do well against the odds.

Joseph and Olivia

Joseph and his sister, Olivia, were admitted to local authority care when they were one and two respectively. Their mother, who had recently emigrated from Africa, suffered increasingly debilitating bouts of mental illness. A year later, when Joseph was just over two years old, the two children were adopted by Christianna who already had birth as well as adopted children. Olivia was not such an easy child. But although she was an 'awkward, moody, unco-operative teenager', she eventually earned herself a degree. In contrast, Joseph was 'a constant delight.' He suffered dyslexia and was a little slow at school. However, he turned out to be a hard working boy who was determined to do well. After attending college, he went out to Nigeria where he started his own business. 'He's a very enterprising young man. Forgetful and untidy, but he likes making money!' He returns home regularly but Christianna says he thoroughly enjoys the life he has made for himself in West Africa.

Amblers

This group of children got by. They appeared contented with life. They never stood out as either brilliant or bad. They seemed to progress through childhood without undue mishap or concern. At school, teachers would usually see them as average, adding 'I wish they'd try a little harder'. Their ambitions were always described as modest but they were usually achieved. They became lorry drivers or shop assistants, bank clerks or full-time mothers, care workers or landscape gardeners. But whatever they did, their parents would invariably describe them as "happy" and "liked by everyone".

Steven

Steven, who was 'an awfully restless baby', became more placid as he got older. At school 'he was the classroom clown, always mucking about.' He could be a bit disruptive in class. One of his senior school reports said 'Steven starts his summer holidays before the rest of the school. He seems to watch cricket more than he watches the blackboard.' But his mother, Jill, said that he had a good sense of humour and was well liked. And as he advanced through his teens, he began to work harder, passing all his 'O' levels . He went through a phase of being interested in his background and on one occasion his parents took him to see where he was born. 'Gosh,' he said, 'Just think. My mother's been in there.' He was always relaxed and at ease about his adoption.

A number of older placed children posed few, if any problems, for their parents.

Al

Al's unmarried birth parents were two very young Asians. Their families refused to let them keep an "illegitimate" child and so Al was placed with foster carers almost from birth. His mother was sent back to India. He was well cared for but when it seemed increasingly unlikely that he would return to his birth parents, he was adopted by Alice. 'He was cuddly, he was lovable and he was deliciously wicked! Full of mischief,' declared Alice. 'He was never any trouble, though I must admit he never worked at school. He had long eyelashes and all he had to do was flutter them at the teachers and he'd get round them. Everyone adored Al. He got a few 'O' levels and went off to Art School at seventeen. He was very successful and is now a leading art director for a London theatre.'

Late starters

Here we meet children who also had happy childhoods. However, school and work definitely took a back seat to friends and fun. It was only by the time they reached their early twenties that they decided it was time to get down to the more serious side of life. In spite of much chivvying and sighs of exasperation from doting parents, school would be "wasted". And yet, given time, all the pieces began to fall together and surprising results, never predicted by teachers, would begin to appear.

Josh

Josh was a black, five week old baby when he was placed with Fay, Charles and their three older children. He was 'a lovely, smiley, happy baby'. He grew up into 'a most loving little boy' though there were times when he did get anxious: 'He liked us to be together all the time. Once when we were on holiday, my husband said he'd go and get the bread. I stayed in the tent to light the camp stove. Josh kept running between us like a little sheep dog trying to keep us together and getting all confused and anxious.' Described as a gentle, friendly child, Fay said that he was 'devoted to her'.

Although everyone saw him as a bright lad, at primary school his teachers would typically say 'We don't think he's stretching himself' and Fay retorted: 'Of course, he wasn't. He was having a happy time with all his friends, coasting along doing just enough to get by.' Fay tried to galvanise him when he went on to secondary school, believing that for a black child to compete successfully 'in that rough, tough bloody old world he would have to be not just better than the next person, but much better.' But 'Josh was not to be galvanised!' Once, aged eleven, having announced he was going to run the London Underground and having just come top in a class intelligence test, Fay said to him: 'Look, you've got good looks and beauty, but your mum's also given you intelligence. Don't waste it! Do something with it!' But throughout his secondary school years, all Fay heard from teachers was that Josh didn't work. 'He's lazy. And all the girls adore him.'

Over the space of a couple of years he stringed together six GCSEs. 'Girls and money' had much more appeal for Josh than 'A' levels. There then followed quite a successful period when he worked in and managed various shops. At twenty one he met a black girl completing a sociology degree. This was his first serious black girlfriend. 'I think it was watching her study that made him chuck in his job and start being academic again, said Fay. 'He's now at the University taking a law degree and he's really enjoying himself.'

Adoption matters

For most parents, there were occasions and incidents when they would be sharply reminded that adopting and being adopted brought extra concerns or made unexpected emotional demands. An unthinking schoolteacher would ask children to draw a family tree or carry out a piece of homework on family genetics. A child would announce that they were going to search for a birth parent and although most adopters willingly supported their son or daughter, they were often surprised how anxious and insecure they could suddenly feel as parents. It seemed that in this group, most adopted children, right up until early adulthood were either 'not particularly interested in their adoption' or simply had a natural curiosity about their background which would sometimes lead, equally naturally, to them searching for one or both of their birth parents. In other words, in most cases adoption was viewed and handled in a relatively relaxed fashion by both parents and children. But there were odd occasions when the meaning of adoption and its implications for relationships and identity were unexpectedly thrown into sharp relief as they intruded into the daily routine of either school or home life.

Roy

Elaine adopted Roy when he was three months old. Roy's birth mother was white and his father was black African. The birth mother's family refused to support their daughter because Roy was a mixed race baby and she felt she had no choice but to give him up for adoption. When Roy was twelve he started biology at school. Elaine described the teacher's first lesson on genetics:

'Roy and two other children were called to the front of the class by the teacher who was intent on demonstrati g some genetic principles. The teacher says to Roy: "Roy, your father I take it is black?" "No," says Roy. "Oh, sorry. Then your mother is black?" "No," says Roy. "Roy, don't be silly. You must be lying!" The stupid woman. She never thought and she accused him of lying. So Roy looks round the class and says: "I'm adopted." And the whole class roared with laughter. He came home really proud of that but even so, we don't know what that cost him, do we?'

Ironically, quite a few adopted children did become very interested in their *adopted* family's history. They became experts on who was who in both past and present generations. Julia believed that, in a sense, Matt adopted them rather than that they had adopted him. 'He became very interested in the family and the wider family. He looked into the history and background of each member, though oddly he wasn't terribly curious about his own adoption or parents.' Interestingly, all the children who developed such an interest were academically extremely able, obtaining first class degrees, becoming doctors or proving to be highly successful in their chosen career.

Most adopters rationally supported any interest their children might show in their birth parents, but emotionally quite a few admitted to having some anxieties. However unlikely, there was that faint fear that they might lose their child. Some adopted children, too, were vaguely unsettled by encouragements to find out more about their birth parent. Their birth parents posed some ill-defined, remote threat that they could lose their adoptive mother and father. 'I don't want to know anything about her; one mother is quite enough,' was one typical retort. 'You're my mum and dad and there is no-one else.' When Rosie wanted to know a lot more about her adoption and her birth mother, Molly was quite happy to tell her and support her. But Paul, who was two years younger than his sister became rather upset at his sister's curiosity. 'Shut up about your adoption,' he shouted at Rosie, 'Mum and Dad are our parents.' Molly said that Paul believed that Rosie was being disloyal.

When Joan's daughter, Debbie, was twenty four, she traced her birth mother. 'It seemed I was the last to know,' said Joan. 'I was really upset. Debbie said she was too frightened to tell us. She'd had counselling first. Then she got in touch with her mother. I was very, very hurt. She was frightened we were going to turn her out. But of course that's one thing we'd never do . . . She found her birth mother in Leeds and went to see her. She said to her that she didn't want another mother but she did want to know her background before starting a family of her own. She was very curious. I was very apprehensive when Debbie went up to Leeds because you don't know what might happen. She satisfied her curiosity. She does keep in touch with her birth mother, but not very regularly. When Debbie got married she came to the wedding. A nice woman. Very quiet. And my goodness, they aren't half alike. Now looking back, I suppose I'm glad she did find her. It seems to have satisfied her curiosity.'

In contrast, many adopters actively supported any interest shown by their children in their adoption, whether it was wanting more information or planning to search for their birth parents. Indeed, in some cases, the adoptive parent was more interested in trying to trace the birth parent than the adopted child.

Philip

Stella was proud of her son, Philip, even as a baby. Throughout his life she had wanted his mother to know how well he was doing. 'When he was a baby, I'd be walking down the street with him in his pram and I'd be looking at every young girl that walked past and I'd be wondering if that was Philip's mother. And I wanted her to see him. I cried the day he started school – "If only she could see him." ' It was the same the day he graduated and got his degree. According to his mother, Philip had never really shown much interest in his adoption. 'If it was ever talked about it was me who brought it up. When he reached eighteen, we gave him all his papers. Then when he was in his early twenties he visited America. His birth mother was Canadian. I told him he really should do something about tracing his birth mother while he was over there because once he was back in Britain it would be very difficult. So I was trying to encourage him. In fact I went so far as to do a big search through all the Canadian telephone directories to come up with some likely names and clues and eventually came up with her address.' When Stella phoned Philip with the news, he was thrilled:

'He said he would write to her. He said he'd tread very carefully. But he didn't get a reply and got very agitated. Then we visited him while he was still working in the States and as I was going on to Canada. I asked Philip if he wanted me to try and make contact with his birth mother and he said "yes." I phoned her and she answered and we were on the phone for an hour. She has three more children. It all poured out. Her children don't know of Philip. She said she had written back to Philip. She wrote again. And then a few weeks later I arranged to meet her. I was weepy, but she wasn't. We went to a coffee bar and spent four or five hours talking. She had never talked to anyone about Philip – ever – about having the baby. I was exhausted. It was all very sad. She had married Philip's birth father but he seemed not to want to know about Philip. She and her husband, she said, never discuss Philip. Can you imagine?

'I was keeping Philip informed of everything. He then came across to Canada with his girlfriend. And he phoned his birth mother. They had a long chat. She said unfortunately she was just about to go away and couldn't see him for some while. Imagine how that poor boy felt having gone half way across the world. Then the next thing was she wouldn't see him. He took it better than me. I was absolutely devastated. I could not believe the woman could do that to him. When I got back to Britain, I phoned her again. I sent her pictures of Philip – as a baby, as a boy, when he graduated. She said her husband wouldn't let him meet her or the other children. She couldn't bring herself to see him. Anyway, Philip has stayed on in California. He's working out there and seems to be doing very well. We see him quite often. He's nearer to them over there. He has a mother and a father and brothers and sisters over there and they're unfinished business. We'll always be his family. I'll have another go next time I'm out there. I'll see her.'

Upsets and disturbances

A few families suffered major upsets of one kind or another. Death or divorce could test both the family's cohesion and the children's emotional strengths. Some parents felt that such traumas, though deeply upsetting, could sometimes bring families even closer together.

Sandra adopted two children – a girl and a boy. Nicole was 'an easy child' who made friends easily. She went through school without any problems. 'She took everything in her stride. I'm making her sound boring but she was an absolutely lovely child.' Her younger brother Alan was more noisy and argumentative. But he, too, was friendly and well-liked. When Nicole was twelve and Alan eight, their father died. Alan 'missed having a father' but both the children were very supportive of their mother at this difficult time. 'When Martin died, I don't think I would have survived without the children,' said Sandra. 'We became very close.'

Divorce could have a slightly more disturbing impact on children. Boys in particular were upset at the departure of their fathers. Ivan's father left the family when he was ten years old. He was very upset. His father had not taken a great deal of interest in Ivan who had been anxious to try and please him. In fact, the day Dyllis went to collect Ivan, her husband had not bothered to join her, claiming he was too busy at work. 'Ivan is now extremely bitter,' said Dyllis. 'He wants nothing to do with his father. He's very resentful and angry that he walked out on us.' But generally, Dyllis described Ivan as a friendly, placid person who is 'quite courageous'. He now works in a bank. Although Ivan's sisters had left home, married and had children, he is twenty seven and still living with his mother. But Dyllis does not mind: 'He's very close to me. Tuned in to me. Very easy to live with. In fact, he's a very nice bloke, my boy!'

David's father also left his family. His experience illustrates the complexities that can began to define some children's familial relationships. They had to handle a varied and subtle range of roles and relationships. 'On the whole I think both the children came through unscathed,' believed Sarah, 'though David can be quite difficult at times. Not long after his father remarried he said "Oh crumbs! Some kids have one mother, some kids have two. But I've got three!" '

Christine's husband left her and their children for another woman. 'It was quite sudden. No warning. All the children found it very sad.' Will was only nine and was close to his father. Although he maintained regular contact, Christine believed that the experience unsettled Will quite badly for several years. She also thought that being adopted compounded Will's anxieties:

'For about a year after the separation, Will was attention-seeking. He would tell quite fantastic stories. He would exaggerate and lie. There was one very elaborate story in which he said a lady had tried to entice him into her car and take him away. I felt he was very insecure really, at that time. He was frightened every time I went out. He would worry if I came home late from a meeting. He'd wait up. I also think his anxieties were tied up with his adoption. He knows his birth mother parted with him and so he must have felt some rejection. Then his dad suddenly walking out – I mean there hadn't been any build up or major rows or anything – that must have added to his insecurity. He was also concerned that I might meet someone else and go off and leave him. I had to keep reassuring him that I would never leave him.'

Looking back

Without exception, adoptive parents of these secure children spoke very positively of their experiences. Many had adopted after years of trying to get pregnant; a few already had birth children before adopting older children. 'An unqualified success,' concluded Geraldine. 'I can't imagine being without Jessica, to be honest,' said Angie. 'Adoption has been wonderful.' 'If I did it again,' ventured Doreen, 'I'd adopt four! Three wasn't enough!'

Kenny had adopted a baby girl when he was working in Vietnam. Lo was in a state orphanage and he knew that if he did not adopt her, she would be destined for the streets and a life of prostitution before she was even in her teens:

'With us, Lo has got a life and she's got a future. But totally selfishly, adopting her has made me feel I've given something back. I'm an ex-children's home kid myself, in trouble, joined the army when I was fifteen. The army treated all the locals in whatever country it found itself like dirt. We screwed their countries and didn't care if we bombed or shot them. And then suddenly, I found myself in a position to put a little back. My only regret is that I didn't bring even more children back with me. Lo has grown up into a wonderful girl and I'm very proud.'

As they reflected on their children and adoption, some parents remembered the birth mother. Their joy, they believed, was at the expense of her sadness. 'The children have been an absolute joy,' said Sandra, 'but you can never quite get out of your head the poor girl who gave them up and what she's missed. You see, now, I have these two beautiful grandchildren and it occurred to me that there is this other woman and she's got them as well, but she doesn't know.'

Thinking about adoption made some parents philosophical. Cathy, who had two birth children before adopting two more, said it made her realise that parents do not "own" their children. 'They are who they are; they are themselves and not who or what you want them to be. Understanding this, I think, has helped me be a better parent to all four children.'

7 Anxious-to-please children

Adopted children whose behaviour throughout childhood indicated that home and family were very important to them but who also showed that they could not quite 'take-them-for-granted' experienced mild feelings of insecurity, albeit at a low level. Anxieties rose whenever parental love, interest or availability appeared in danger of being lost, at least as perceived by the child. This meant that anxious children were a little vulnerable to the inevitable ups and downs of life – changes of school, moves of house, parental exasperation, academic setbacks, failed friendships. Although they were reasonably confident of their parents' love, they never quite assumed its unconditional availability in the way that totally secure children did. There was a vague, background worry that in relationships they might, once again, be rejected and suffer hurt. But overall, these were happy, rewarding children who were loved unreservedly by their parents. Their adoptions were successful and they entered adulthood with growing confidence.

Children who remained mildly anxious throughout their childhood might have been placed at any age. However, it seemed rare for children placed as very young babies to follow this pattern. More typical of this group were children placed as older babies at around six or seven months, children placed as toddlers often with a short history of abuse or neglect, and children placed after the age of four who had experienced some love and care, but which in the end turned out to be unreliable and inconsistent. The older the child was at the time of placement, the higher was the level of insecurity.

The children described as "anxious" shared a number of common behaviours and characteristics. There were subtle differences depending on the children's age at placement, but the underlying theme was one of mild insecurity, a lack of confidence and slight emotional immaturity.

From the baby's or child's point of view, it seemed that the care and love they received before they were adopted was sound and reliable, but in spite of anything they did or tried to do, that secure relationship was suddenly lost – a parent might have become mentally ill, or a mother might have entered a new relationship in which the step-father rejected the child in favour of his own children. Such an event was guaranteed to upset any feelings of self-confidence the children were beginning to develop. It seemed to these children that emotionally important relationships could never again be wholly assumed or taken for granted. Most of the adopters were instinctively aware of this and could empathise with their children, even though there were times when the insecurities of their sons or daughters produced exasperating behaviour.

The loss of secure and safe relationships hovered as an ever present possibility in the children's lives – 'it has happened before and so it could happen again.' So when any situation arose that seemed to threaten the loss of the close attachment that the children felt they had with their adoptive parents, such as mother going into hospital or a major change in the family's routine, then the children's level of anxiety rose. We might conclude that these children had experienced some love and affection in their initial relationships and therefore knew what they were missing. Placed in their new families, they were keen to "fit in" and try their best. In most relationships, these children were anxious-to-please.

As they grew up, the children were keen to establish close relationships but were extra-sensitive to any perceived lack of interest or rejection, even when none was present or intended. When they felt insecure, they became anxious. And when they were anxious they could become fragile, tearful, irritable, fretful, impatient, demanding, attention-seeking and confused. People, including parents and teachers, often described them as "immature". They could be silly and liable to "show-off". When they calmed down and realised they had been "childish", they sought reassurance and would seek to make amends. But they were also very loving children who were keen to be loved.

'Naughty but nice' was how Bryony described her son. However, "naughty" was not quite the right word. These children got into trouble through thoughtlessness and being silly or "daft". Because they were keen to keep in with their friends, they would either show off or be foolish enough to do what someone "dared" them to do. They did not intend to misbehave as such, but rather they were keen to be accepted. Such immaturity meant that the more mature children did not find them very satisfying or sensible friends. There was therefore a tendency to end up in peer groups in which behaviour was less mature and less responsible.

Other complaints from teachers and parents included a lack of concentration, a proneness to lose things and to be very untidy, and a general scattiness. However, these were well-meaning children. They did not steal or get into criminal trouble. They remained anxious to keep their parents' love, even though their behaviour sometimes exasperated and exhausted mothers and fathers. They were often generous and could be quite sentimental. In many cases these children would be the last to leave home. They seemed to need a few extra years to grow up and feel fully confident about assuming independence. Children had lingering worries that when they did leave home, mum and dad might stop loving them. Therefore separation was difficult. While brothers and sisters would be off at college or moving to a new job in a distant city or getting married, these more anxious children would still be at home in their mid-twenties. There were also hints that whereas anxious boys tended to behave in an outwardly disorganised way, anxious girls were inclined to be more clingy and compliant when young and occasionally more moody and withdrawn for a while in their teens.

But these were likeable children. Parents always spoke warmly of them. And without exception, mothers and fathers viewed the adoption fondly and positively.

Backgrounds and beginnings

The anxiety felt by these children manifested itself from the outset. They had not been so hurt by the adult world that they had become implacably hostile or had switched off emotionally, but they did not entirely trust people to be interested in them or consistently responsive. They wanted to love and be loved but they lacked that inner security which allowed them to take these things for granted. When Marjorie and Kevin looked back at old photographs of Stacey they could see 'that slightly apprehensive look in her eyes. She was such a timid little girl.'

Upon arrival, the children reacted in one of three ways: they became clingy; they felt confused and agitated; or they tested their new parents.

Clingers

This group almost literally clung to their new parents, never letting them out of their sight. Having experienced some affection and lost it, they seemed determined not to lose love a second time. Melissa was received into care at the age of six months after her mother took an overdose. She cried all the time while she was with her foster carers. Several days later, she returned to her mother but there were continued worries about her care, including some suspicions that Melissa and her older brother were being sexually abused. She was placed for adoption with Patricia at the age of twenty months. 'When she came, Melissa latched on to me like a little limpet. She decided she liked me and that's where she remained for the next two years; firmly attached. She followed me around everywhere. Wouldn't let go. She screamed if I went out of sight. She slept in our bed for many years. Always on my side of the bed though. She was – still is – wary of men.'

Another group of "anxious" children generally joined their families at the age when they were toddlers. They had been badly physically abused during their first few months of life. Periods in hospital and foster care preceded their adoption. The damage and injuries caused by the abuse meant that the adopters found themselves providing physical and emotional care of a high intensity. The result was that parents were brought into repeated close and intimate contact with their children from the moment they arrived. This need for close, intense physical involvement seemed to accelerate the attachment process and bring children and parents very close together.

Flora's birth mother was eighteen when she was born. From the beginning, Flora had a history of bruising. She cried a great deal. It seemed that both parents were responsible for her injuries. As a baby Flora suffered a fractured skull which caused partial paralysis and convulsions. The hospital also discovered fractured ribs, an eye injury and old cigarette burns. She spent several months in hospital before being placed at the age of fifteen months with Elaine, her husband and their two young children. 'We had to invest an awful lot of time and love with Flora. She needed a vast amount of physical care, encouragement and emotional support. But against all the medical predictions, we got her to walk and be a normal little girl. The surgeon said it was a miracle the way she had turned out.'

Eddy is hemiplegic but his mobility, with a raised boot, was quite good. He had been in a children's home for several years and when he was ten years old he was adopted by Marian and her husband:

'He was so good when he arrived, almost too good to be true! If you said "Sit" he'd sit. He was like a little zombie at first. Incredibly anxious to please all the time. But he also wanted a lot of affection and attention. He wanted to know where I was all the time. And wherever he went, he would tell me where he was going. "I'm going to the toilet now!" he would shout. "I'm going to play in the garden now." He'd tell me at least three times that he was going to play in the garden before he actually went! And everything, sort of, had to be a routine. But once he arrived, he never looked back. Wonderful boy.'

The agitated

These children needed to be won over before they could allow them-selves to love and be loved. They almost had to be forced to relax and relate – the parents offered an instinctive form of "holding therapy". But the children quickly succumbed. Rachel, for example, who had spent over a year in a highly regimented residential nursery, 'couldn't even choose things for herself for tea,' said Alice,

'She had to have things put on her plate. She was like this for months. Inside her shell. Then I produced Jane and I used to get Rachel to help me with this new baby. And gradually she became very helpful. She loved to look after Jane. I would also pick Rachel up and plonk her on my lap and gradually it all began to work. I made her come and cuddle us in our bed in the morning. And she started to come alive. And slowly, she began to smile.'

Nancy

Nancy's mother was fifteen when she was born. The young woman stayed at home with her parents and although very fond of the child, she treated Nancy more like a baby sister than a daughter. When Nancy was three years old, her mother married and soon had two more children. Her stepfather was hostile and rejected Nancy. When she came home from school, she was sent straight up to her bedroom and was not allowed to play with her younger half-sisters. She also had to have her tea in her bedroom, on her own. Nancy's mother joined in the rejection. She said to Petra, Nancy's adoptive mother: 'The more Nancy tried to please us, the more we seemed to dislike her.' Social workers then tried respite care for Nancy. But when she returned home the rejection was as strong as ever. At age eight, Nancy was adopted by Petra:

'At first I didn't think it was going to work. She was over-effusive with our older boys. When we took her out, she was a real harum-scarum. We took her for a walk and she jumped in a little pond. I thought "Oh my God!" Nancy was really hyperactive. I came back from that walk thinking "We're never going to be able to cope with that girl." It was my son, Seb, who made me think how Nancy must have felt – new house, new family, new everything. But she settled down by the end of the week. She became one of us. She always wanted to be by my side. Wanted to help with the washing up, the cooking, the cleaning. She seemed to be always smiling at that time as if she was always trying to please us. She was so anxious to please. Whatever I was doing she wanted to do it for me. She wanted to know how to make a cup of tea when she saw the boys make me one . . .

'Very quickly she became very, very tidy. If she was told something, she took it to the letter. "Keep your bedroom tidy" and immaculately tidy it would be. "You'll need to get some clothes out for school tomorrow" and everything would be there, neat and tidy . . .

'She followed Seb and me all over the place. Even if I went to the loo, she'd be there! If I went in the bath, Nancy would jump in with me. After a couple of months, we said to her "You can call us what you like, you know – Petra, Tim, whatever" and one night after I'd put her to bed and I was just going down the stairs, she said "Goodnight . . . Goodnight, Mum." I rushed back up the stairs and really cuddled her. And I said "Oh, darling, that's really nice," and she said "Well, you are my mum." '

The testers

Some children who had experienced many changes of caretaker *after* the age of two or three, along with a confusing mix of good times and bad, arrived in their new homes awkward, cross and angry. They had experienced times when they were loved and times when they were neglected. Their initial behaviour was difficult and testing. They seemed to be saying 'Look, I'm not at all sure that you really want me, so I'll test you out. I will misbehave and show no gratitude.' There was much toddler-like defiance: 'Shan't! Won't! Make me!' But their need to be wanted was apparent even when they were being difficult and provocative. If the adopters passed this test, the children relaxed and seemed to accept – or almost accept – that they belonged. They became much more settled and responsive. Elements of insecurity remained, but parents experienced very few problems once the children began to trust their new parents and believed that they really had made a long-term commitment. The testing phase could last months or even a couple of years, but the eventual outcome saw a relative calm and loving relationship establish itself between parents and children.

Henry

Henry's mother was seventeen years old at the time of his birth. While she went out to work, Henry was looked after by her boyfriend, Pete, although he was not the boy's father. By all accounts he coped well with the baby. Henry remembered Pete with affection and was very upset to lose him at the age of three. When Henry reached the age of five, his mother and new boyfriend had a baby. The relationship between the young couple then fell into conflict and Henry's mother appeared to have made her eldest son the scapegoat for all her ills.

Henry's behaviour became disruptive, disturbed and aggressive. His mother married her new boyfriend and Henry's behaviour deteriorated further. Violence by his new stepfather led to Henry being received into care for short periods. At the age of six he went into a long-term foster home because his mother 'feared for his safety'. She promised to visit him, but often failed to appear, upsetting Henry even further. His excitement at impending visits was followed by rage when she did not turn up. He tore his clothes and destroyed his favourite toys. After one year, Henry's foster mother's marriage broke up. The decision was made to place Henry for adoption. By now he was seven years old.

There was a long introductory period before he joined Hannah and Harry. They had no other children. During his visits, Henry would get 'over-excited' and 'behave terribly'. 'We took him to the zoo on one occasion,' said Harry, 'and he played up something rotten. I think he made his mind up saying "This is me. This is what you get. Let's see what you make of me." And he was an absolute devil. Other people looking at us must have wondered what kind of parents we were not controlling that little horror! If you said "Come here!" he would walk off in the opposite direction. He had an old brown anorak and he would wriggle his arm out of his sleeve so you couldn't hold hands with him. His sleeve was left dangling so we were left holding an empty sleeve! Everything that day was "No. Don't want to do that. Don't want to be here." By the end of the day, we were wrecks.'

And when he first arrived for good 'it was testing, testing the whole time,' said Hannah. 'When I bathed him, I'd run the water and he'd pull the plug out. I'd put the plug back in, then he'd pull it out again. And then when I said it was time to come out of the bath, he'd refuse. By the end of that first week, we were drained [sic!].'

But even during these testing times Henry would show and want lots of affection. 'He'd sit on my lap,' said Hannah, 'and he loved a rough and tumble with Harry on the floor . . . You could tell he loved the physical contact.' He loved having stories read to him. And yet, next minute he would be just as awkward as ever. 'Even so,' added Hannah, 'we had no doubts. I liked him from the moment I saw him.' 'He'd got a lovely little face,' said Harry. 'He's a lovely looking boy. He fitted in. It was easy to see through the naughtiness. He was just a little boy crying for help.'

Harry and Hannah were confirmed in this belief when, two months after Henry had joined them, he began to enjoy "regressing".

'After a bath, he would love to be wrapped up in his big bath towel and act like a baby. He would laugh and go "ga! ga!" He thought this was smashing. There was one occasion when he was in his big bath towel when he suddenly got sad. He said he wanted to go back to Southampton where he had come from. He asked to be taken to the front door. He said he wanted a label put on him so he could be posted. And Harry took him out the front door and then brought him in the back. And we said "We don't really want you to go. We can't do it." And that was a turning point. It was as if he was saying to us "I like it here. But I know you're going to send me back one day, so let's get it over with." And after that, he didn't want to be a baby anymore. And he was less sad.'

Access and contested adoptions

The placement of older children also witnessed a rise in the number of contested adoptions. Some children removed from parents who had been found guilty of abusing them, discovered that their parents not only fought the adoption but also attempted to maintain contact. Most adopters found both the contact and the contest very stressful. All claimed that their children were upset by the continued visits of the birth parents. It seemed to them that their children's insecurity was being perpetuated by mothers and fathers who insisted on seeing their sons and daughters. Elaine recalls:

'I found Flora's contact with her mother very difficult. While Flora was still being fostered, her mother visited every two weeks. It was a most fraught situation for me. I found it so difficult to see this young woman bouncing Flora up and down on her knee knowing that she had caused her so much physical damage and injury. She seemed to show no remorse at all. She was a loud woman with peroxide blond hair and big legs and I found her just too much. The birth mother appealed against the adoption and was successful. The judge said it looked as if she was getting her life back together again. We'd had her for well over a year by then. I was absolutely devastated. We had had good contact with Flora's paternal grandparents and we told them of the decision. They were outraged and phoned social services and told them more of the abuse that Flora had suffered. They were frightened for Flora and couldn't think of her going back to her mother. Our solicitor told us we had no choice but to comply. But then we got on to The National Association of Foster Parents. They put us on to their legal advisor and she was marvellous. She said these provincial solicitors knew nothing of the law. We got Flora made a Ward of Court. All very traumatic. The stress at this time was relentless. We were fortunate in having the support of friends and our local church.

'And all the time we had the access visits, Flora went down hill. She would cling to the door jambs shouting "Don't make me go mummy, don't make me go, please!" Carol, her mother, would be pulling her and I would try to prise her fingers off the door. We had no choice. The courts said we'd be in trouble if we didn't co-operate. Eventually Flora began to get physically ill. She'd have stomach pains on the morning of the visit. She'd have night terrors. After medical advice and intervention we did eventually manage to get the access visits stopped. What a relief! Flora picked up quickly once the nightmare was over. The birth mother contested the adoption in court but it failed. Our solicitor was wonderful. Brilliant. But it was an awful, awful time.'

The long-term legacies of early insecurities

Once the children had settled into their new family life, parents began to recognise the behaviours and traits that were to become typical of their son or daughter. The unsettled months and years left their mark on the children's confidence. Insecure feelings were easily roused whenever there was stress or upset. The children tended to be home-centred. Some were shy and not sure of themselves in social situations. They tried, but did not always succeed, to be good. There was an anxiety to please and be liked. This made them extra-sensitive to other people's moods and feelings. The children also tended to have a particular sympathy for people and animals who were vulnerable, dependent or in need of protection. Pets would be looked after. They liked babies. And often they would find careers in one of the caring professions. But the desire to be liked and accepted by family and friends made some children, especially boys, prone to show off and be silly.

"Anxious-to-please" children liked harmony. Upsets to routines unsettled them. They were children who always tried hard, whether at home or school. But their lack of confidence and sometimes lack of concentration meant that they did not always do as well as perhaps they should.

Not surprisingly, given this array of characteristics, these were likable children. And as the years went by, the children's trust in their parents and belief in themselves slowly grew. The underlying anxiety never quite left them, but on the whole these children enjoyed happy childhoods and successful placements.

The legacy of early upsets and losses was seen most vividly in five areas of the children's personal make-up and psychology: feeling anxious, eating too much, not coping well with change, a general anxiety to please, and a wish to belong. By no means did all children display behaviours in each and every one of these areas, but the children's underlying feelings of insecurity were easily recognised and spotted by sympathetic and understanding parents. The behaviours most frequently described by mothers and fathers to illustrate their children's insecurities included shyness, lack of confidence, poor concentration, scattiness, proneness to accidents, fear of scrutiny and public exposure (for example, taking exams and having to talk to the whole class at school), and a preference for the familiar and routine.

Feeling anxious

Feeling anxious and uncertain affected children in a variety of ways. Nancy was anxious every time her parents had visitors. 'She wouldn't leave the room,' explained Petra, 'She said she was worried about what they might say about her if she wasn't there. I suppose it must have felt a bit like the conversations that her parents and social worker had about what to do about her when she was younger which would lead to her being removed each time.'

Eating too much

The insecurity and anxiety felt by some children resulted in uncontrolled eating. When they felt worried or frightened, they ate and ate. Trudy went to live with Peggy when she was five. She had lived with her mother and grandparents until she was two and seemed to have been loved and well cared for. Then her mother had another baby and her parents were no longer prepared to have her live at home. Life went rapidly downhill for Trudy. She suffered neglect. Her mother had a series of boyfriends and there were suspicions she might have been physically abused. Peggy said:

'When she came to live with us, it was as if she was thinking to herself "Well, I've got the good things back again and I'm not letting them go." She was desperate to be adopted. But when she first came, she ate like a pig. She just could not get enough food down her fast enough. And then she would get on the floor and look for the crumbs. Food was always an obsession with Trudy. It's not that she was hungry. She just couldn't stop. For a long time she raided the pantry. I had to put a lock on it in the end. She'd eat the school lunches I'd prepared the night before and I'd come down in the morning and all the lunches would be gone. It was a very stressful time. Food is still something of a problem with her, even now, at twenty.'

Coping with change and reacting to upset
The children in this group were desperate for stability. Any disturbance or change in routine could act as a reminder of more troubled times. Their anxieties would break to the surface and it would be a while before feelings of security would return. Holidays, regarded as a treat by parents, caused many children to become agitated and difficult. Some children took months or years to settle after a house move or a change of school.

The particularly insecure children became upset over very minor things. Not being able to find a pair of shoes, the wrong towel being in the bathroom, or the replacement of an old bed could easily trigger tears and a temper. However, these upsets would be short-lived. More disturbing were major alterations in daily routine. When Greg was twelve, Connie fell seriously ill with meningitis. He had arrived at the age of five and had always been 'a happy-go-lucky fellow and such a lovely, loving little boy.' Connie was whisked off to hospital. 'Poor Greg was absolutely distraught. He planned to leave home. He thought I was going to die, you see. He made contingency plans. He got a food supply ready and he was going to take off. He was so frightened at the prospect of losing me, he told me afterwards. Ever since – and he's now twenty two and lives nearby – he sees me or phones me two or three times a week to make sure I'm all right!'

Anxious to please

As both children and adults, the people in this group remained attentive and thoughtful. The phrase "anxious to please" was used again and again by parents. The children wanted to "fit in". Guy, for example, was described by his mother as 'a bit of a chameleon; very loving and totally delightful, but anxious to fit in.' As children, they tended to be compliant and rarely put up much resistance, preferring to accommodate and defuse. Sita, a girl of Indian ethnic background, was adopted by an Indian family when she was eight years old. 'When Sita was asked a question, she'd always try and answer what she thought people wanted to hear. She would prefer to listen and try to blend in . . . She'd spend hours washing up and if she broke a cup, she'd run upstairs and hide and get right under the bed. She was never naughty. Never caused any trouble. Sita was always worried that we'd be cross with her.'

It was not unusual, especially during the first years of the placement, for some children to need to make constant declarations of love. Many of the children had a strong sentimental streak. They would be good at remembering everyone's birthday and would make exaggerated responses on Mother's Day and at Christmas. Nancy was always writing her mother notes which said things like 'Mum – I love you lots and lots.'

'Lucille is a great one for birthday cards and loving messages,' said Colette. 'She likes to keep things happy and on an even keel. She's got a sunny, happy personality and doesn't like things to go up and down.'

The wish to keep everyone smiling was linked with the children's extra sensitivity to other people's moods and feelings, particularly their parents. 'Sandy would do anything to keep the peace,' said Joan. 'She was a sweetie. She was very clingy and very dependent on me. Very anxious to please. And very anxious that I should be happy. Even now I can hardly look in any mood without Sandy asking "What's wrong Mum?"'

Wanting to belong

Changing names was a symbolic and meaningful act for a number of these children. 'From the day he arrived at the age of six,' said Vera, 'Tommy insisted on calling himself Tommy Johnson – our surname. All his clothes had to have labels with his new name in them. It was highly significant to him. He seemed to be saying, "This is where I now belong, and you won't be able to shift me that easily." '

Name changes, too, could confirm acceptance and add to a child's feelings of security. When Henry joined his family, he was originally named Darren. His father, Harry, tells the following story:

'After he'd been with us about three or four months, we were watching a school play and this woman sitting near asked him his name – which then, of course, was Darren. He said nothing. And I said "Tell the lady your name." Nothing. So I said to her, "It's Darren." And he said "No it's not!" Well, this woman looked at me most strange. So I said, "Well it was Darren when we came in." Then he said, "It's not now." So I said "What is it, then?" And he said "Harry" which of course is my name. "Oh," I said, "I think we better talk about this later." Well, he said he didn't like the name Darren any more and he wanted to be Harry. Hannah said "Well, we've already got one Harry in the house, and it will be very confusing to have two." And so for a whole week he was nothing! His friends would come to the door and ask to play with Darren and he would shout "Darren's not in!" We got a book with lots of names and he said he quite liked the name Henry which was quite like Harry. He asked us each in turn if we liked it and we said yes. "Well then," he said, "I'm Henry." '

School and the middle years

School was rarely a serious problem. Although some children were a bit disorganised, scatty and attention-seeking, many others were systematic and hardworking. Only a few, like Greg, never really got down to study: 'He had a very strong play instinct,' said his mother, 'and work always got in the way of fun. He was very sociable and the teachers, even though they got exasperated with him, were fond of Greg.' Most of the children were liked by their teachers and they would often want to help in the classroom. However, there was a fear of failure. Some children would try and avoid testing situations. They might be unwell on the day of an exam or perform below their ability in order to stay with work they knew they could do. Chas 'was terrified of failure'. Although he was bright, he avoided situations in which he might not perform well. Whenever there was an exam at school or college:

'. . . he simply would not turn up. He took a catering course. He was brilliant at the practical work, but he never managed to sit any of the written papers just because he was afraid he would fail. Even interviews for jobs were a problem. He worked himself up so much before hand, that very often he never turned up. He may have been eighteen, but inside he was like a little nine-year-old boy.'

The children seemed to cope best with schools that offered clear structures, solid routines and caring staff. If the boundaries were too loose and the style too permissive, these children lost their bearings, became very disruptive, and failed to do well. Indeed, parent after parent of these children spoke of the need to offer them a strong mix of affection and discipline, love and control, physical contact and clear boundaries. Without the strong structures, whether at home or school, the children would feel insecure and anxious and their behaviour would rapidly deteriorate.

Gary found school too demanding and over-stimulating for quite a while. He would show off with his friends who would goad him into doing silly things. On one occasion he was dared to write "bugger off" with a felt tip on a teacher's car. He was caught and punished with detention for a week. Although quite a clever boy himself, he would always play with the less academically able children who, like him, were immature.

'He was impulsive. Always act first and never think through what he was doing. He craved approval and attention and it would get him into trouble time and again. He never seemed to learn. If the others smoked, so would he. If anyone teased him, he'd get wild and throw his schoolbooks just as the teacher walked into the room. That kind of thing, all the time. But then at fifteen, he suddenly seemed to settle a lot more. Grew up and actually became quite sensible and did surprisingly well in his exams.'

Carl

Carl joined Vicky's family when he was four weeks old. Throughout his childhood 'he would test boundaries an awful lot and play up much more than his older brothers and sisters. Mischievous is the word that comes to mind, but nothing ever serious.' As a toddler, Vicky described him as 'affectionate, fiery and outgoing – and very attached to me.' Carl 'never took school work too seriously.' He enjoyed school and was very sociable, but the teachers always saw him as lazy. 'But he has brains, though he doesn't always use them.' He was slow to read, more because of a lack of interest than an inability. When he went to senior school, Carl would get into odd bits of silly trouble that would annoy the teachers. 'For instance, on one occasion he poked a Bunsen burner down the laboratory sink and pumped it full of gas and then lit it. There was a huge explosion. The chemistry teacher was not amused. Carl's naughtiness has always been more spectacular than any of the others.' He struggled to pass a couple of 'O' levels when he was sixteen.

Adolescence into adulthood

Parents could suffer the usual ups and downs with their teenage sons and daughters, but relationships between them always remained basically good. There were never any serious worries or issues. Indeed, the children gradually gained in confidence. Emotionally they could still be a little immature. In most cases this was most clearly revealed in the children's reluctance to leave home until they were well into their twenties. They seemed to need a few extra years to seal their relationship and feel absolutely confident in the permanence of the parent–child tie.

A not uncommon pattern was for the young person to find a flat, give up and return home after a few months before trying again. These hesitant, trial leavings might continue over a two or three year period. In general, the age at which these children left home tended to be older than some of their more secure counterparts. Having arrived late, they intended to leave late.

Caring natures

The children's wish to be liked and accepted revealed itself in certain regularly encountered personality traits. Parents would typically describe their children as 'lovely natured', 'caring and sensitive', 'a worrier who liked everyone to be happy'. The caring side would express itself in a love of animals and a concern for vulnerable people.

The children's caring, protective and nurturing natures also influenced career choices. Working with people or working with food were popular first jobs. Nadine had arrived, aged four, 'a withdrawn, very quiet little girl,' said Joan. Everyone always liked Nadine. She left school and eventually gained a social sciences degree. 'She always wanted to work with children,' continued Joan. And after travelling and finding various child care jobs around the world, she trained and qualified as a social worker. At twenty eight she lives in the same town as her mother and works for the local social services department with children. She had been in care herself as a little girl. Nadine, who had appeared on a television programme about adoption, had reflected much on her own experiences and recognised how they had affected her personality and behaviour: 'I think the early years left their mark,' she said. 'There are still very few people outside my family that I would trust with anything that was important to me. I can be flippant with people at times and that's a defensive barrier because I don't like people to get close to me because I think deep down I'm just waiting for them to hurt me, leave me, abandon me.'

The other side of anxious children's personalities was their great awareness of other people's moods and feelings. However, this wanting to please, accommodate and be loved could get the girls into difficulties in their teens. Several of these "anxious" adolescents found themselves involved with boys to the extent of getting pregnant. Carmel 'was for ever anxious to please,' said Molly. 'Washing up, tidying up around the house. She needed to be a good girl and she was longing for a home and a family of her own. But when she was sixteen she got a boyfriend and in no time at all she was pregnant. She had an abortion. Then at seventeen she was pregnant again, but this time she had a miscarriage.'

Searching
Having experienced insecurity when cared for by their birth mothers and then finding security in adoption, these children were reluctant, anxious

or even hostile to the idea of renewing contact with their mothers. Searching and tracing were rare, at least until the children had reached their mid-twenties and felt more confident and secure in themselves.

'When I was talking to Greg once about his mother, he really cut me short. He said "Listen Mum, you're the best mum I've ever had" and with that the topic had to be dropped. He's now in his twenties and he has never considered getting in touch with her.'

Moira told her adoptive mother, Marilyn, that she had no desire to see her birth mother. 'She said to me, "I wish people would stop going on about it." It really made her cross.'

Hints of anger, generally rare with these children, occasionally tinged the anxiety. Nadine, now in her late twenties and working with children herself, told Joan 'I have no wish to see my birth mother. I really do not understand how any woman can give a child up.'

Nancy was more typical. Trying to understand being given up by her birth mother, she told Petra 'I think she was too young at the time really to be able to look after me.' With Petra's encouragement, she has received communications from her maternal grand-mother, who was opposed to the adoption, but 'she is not ready to reciprocate. She likes to know she's there, but Nancy isn't ready to make direct contact even with her grand-mother yet. It's all too unsettling, I think.'

Looking back

Without exception, the adopters of these children reviewed their progress with great satisfaction and pleasure. They spoke positively of their now grown-up sons and daughters. The children's lurking feelings of insecurity always meant that they were keen to remain emotionally close to their parents. And although their anxieties and behaviour were sometimes exasperating, especially in the case of boys, they were rewarding to love. Anxious to please and desperate to belong, these children were impossible not to like. Vulnerabilities remained, but all were enormously strengthened by their adoptions. With enthusiastic children and responsive parents, benign circles quickly became the order of the day:

'I've had more happiness with the children than anybody has a right to expect. I think if you take children for what they are and not for what you want them to be – enjoy them for themselves – then that's what they want. They want to be wanted.

'Love is its own reward. That's why we took the children. We didn't ask for anything from them. There is satisfaction in giving and we have no right to expect anything in return. If you expect returns, you may well – indeed, you probably certainly will – be disappointed.'

8 Angry children

Whereas adopted children who felt mildly insecure became more anxious if their relationships with significant others seemed threatened, the children we meet in this group expressed their anxiety in the form of anger and hostility. Their anger was directed at those closest to them. The disruptions which they had experienced in their first few weeks, months and years of life left them feeling resentful and irritable. They wriggled, fought and rejected any attempts at renewed intimacy and close contact. It was as if children in this group sensed that life's early rhythms had been profoundly disturbed and that the natural and expected order had been fundamentally upset. During adolescence their anger, irritability and frustration was directed at either the adoptive parents (who appeared as a consequence of the disruption) or the birth mother (who seemed to be the cause of the disruption) or both. Sometimes, the children's hostilities were directed solely at the adopters in which case the birth mother was seen as an innocent party as well as a romanticised, ideal parent.

And yet these feelings of anger were also mixed with feelings of confusion and insecurity. The important thing to note is that the children remained wholly *preoccupied* with their close relationships. Children could feel a deep ambivalence towards their adoptive parents. They could feel hostile to their mothers and fathers because they were not their birth parents; they could show anger because they were disturbed in infancy; they could experience fear that no-one really loved them; they could suffer anxiety because they wanted to be held and comforted and yet could not seem to stop themselves being cross and difficult. They found it hard to let go of their parents and yet could not stop attacking them, emotionally, verbally and even physically. It was as if they had had something taken away and they were now flailing about helplessly and hopelessly trying to recover it. The intimacy they wanted *was* being offered by their adoptive parents, but confusingly these people were also not their birth parents. In some odd way, it felt as if they were the adults who had deprived them of their original family. And yet the adopters were the only people who had consistently loved the children and the only people available to be loved by the children. The adopters were therefore the most important and valuable people in the children's lives as well as being the only people at whom the children could direct all their anger, confusion and bewilderment. Hence the children's agitated preoccupation with their parents.

A number of children said they felt that they 'didn't belong' or fit in their families. And for those who had brothers or sisters, especially younger brothers and sisters, it was extremely common for parents to report that the "angry" child was "very jealous" of the sibling. Some of these anxieties manifested themselves in problems over food. Not all children exhibited eating problems, but the numbers were certainly much higher than average. Food could become a weapon. It could be used to symbolise the giving and withholding of affection. Refusing food was equivalent to rejecting the love being offered.

When they reached adulthood, these children rarely disappeared totally out of the lives of their parents. If they left home precipitately and in angry mood, they often returned a few months or even years later as if nothing had happened. They continued to demand as they had demanded throughout their childhoods. They wanted demonstrations and constant proof that they were loved and wanted. But it did not seem to matter how much love or attention was given, they never seemed able to accept it or be satisfied. Occasionally these long episodes of tension and dispute were punctuated by spells of affectionate calm in which the child sought to get close, both physically and emotionally. However, overall this was an exhausting formula for the parents – to give and give without any let up in the demands. It is not surprising therefore that many adoptive parents with such children reached a stage when they felt that the child or young adult just had to leave the home. Marriages came under strain, parents felt desperate, and brothers and sisters suffered.

The anger became more pronounced as the child advanced through adolescence. Many children lied extensively and excessively. Deceit and deviousness further distorted and damaged relationships between parents and child. Some children began to steal money from home, particularly and pointedly from their parents. A few boys became violent and developed an interest in weapons. Some girls started having sex in their early teens with a series of boyfriends; relationships were usually short-term and pregnancies were not uncommon. They became "wild" and unruly. 'She seemed to have a self-destruct button,' was how one parent described her daughter.

The more confused and frustrated children began to commit crimes outside the home, take drugs and generally slip on a downward slope of despair and outrage. They no longer seemed to care what was happening to them. This attitude was tied up in some confusing way with feelings of early rejection: 'I was not wanted or loved so maybe I'm not likeable or lovable'; 'No-one cared for me so I don't care what happens to me.' These children experienced more profound feelings of anxiety and insecurity than those described as "anxious to please" in the previous chapter.

During these difficult days, school work suffered. The children lacked the ability to concentrate. Many played truant. Teachers complained that the children were disinterested or disruptive. Exams were failed and few children gained more than a handful of weak academic passes. Significantly, if a parent had an interest in a particular academic subject, the child did least well in that exam. Children of vicars failed Religious Studies. If a parent taught Chemistry or History, marks in those subjects would be lowest of all. And yet many of these children, *particularly those adopted as young babies*, were described as very bright and clever by their parents. Parents regularly described their children as having high IQs as well as "difficult" and "demanding" temperaments. More than any other group, parents were likely to see their children as creative or artistic, talented or musical. But few of these early promises were realised in the form of successes at school or beyond. Compared to their secure counterparts, few made it into higher education or university.

The majority were also described as "strong characters", "stubborn" or "wilful" by their parents. This may simply have meant that any child who stood out and confronted adults was likely to be called "strong" or "wilful". Or it might have indicated that a particular combination of good intelligence and demanding temperament produced feelings of anger in those who found themselves in disturbed and disrupted situations. Feelings of anger and frustration were particularly likely to arise in children who had some kind of awareness of what was happening (because of their intelligence, cognitive sensitivities and social alertness) but who were unable to do anything about it. Feelings of impotence and helplessness arose out of such experiences. It may have seemed to these children that in spite of their protests, caregiving relationships were lost, changed and swapped without reference to their wants and feelings in the matter.

Out of such relationship histories emerged personalities which were demanding and attention-seeking. Many found it difficult to make and keep friends. Their behaviour and personality often meant that they were not popular children with their peers. Some children found it difficult and distressing to cope with change. House moves, changes of school, new teachers and upsets in familiar routines easily tipped them up. Situations in which the children felt exposed or challenged increased feelings of insecurity. The children reacted badly, often with aggression, anger and irritability. Parents tried not to rock the boat, but upsets could not always be avoided or anticipated. For example, these children rarely travelled well. Holidays would trigger awkwardness. 'Over the years,' said Elma, 'Susie would never cope with journeys and suitcases and any sort of suggestion of going anywhere. She would be tense and disturbed and surly about going away. She'd be thoroughly unpleasant and just could not handle it.' And it was these children too, who were most likely to be extremely untidy, disorganised and prone to lose things.

Most "angry" children had dealings at one time or another with either a child psychiatrist or an educational psychologist. However, it was rare for a parent to report positively on these professional encounters. Many parents felt they were being blamed by the experts for their child's problems. This only added to their already strong feelings of guilt and despair. For example, Karl had behaved so badly at school and claimed that he hated home so much, Arnold and Lydia finally agreed to send him to boarding school. However, he continued to truant, run away and get into trouble with teachers. The school encouraged Karl's parents to have him seen by a psychologist. 'She was very hard on us,' said Lydia. 'She kept saying "This poor child. It's absolutely criminal for you to send an adopted child away to boarding school." We felt it was all our fault and not down to him at all. We were made to feel useless parents. We felt so awful and so guilty it made matters ten times worse.' Other parents simply felt that the psychiatrists and psychologists they saw were either "useless" or "a complete waste of time".

But for most parents, if they were patient, there was light at the end of the tunnel. The children's anger would finally abate. What triggered this varied from case to case. It might be that a birth mother was traced and so a particular ghost was laid to rest. Leaving home and getting a clearer perspective on life helped. Meeting a loving and supportive partner gave some adopted adults that final dose of confidence and self-regard. And having a child of their own often helped dissipate anger. Perhaps one of the most important ingredients was the willingness of some parents to stick with their difficult and demanding children "through thick and thin". Not to give up on them seemed to be the most powerful therapy; that in spite of everything that the children had thrown at their parents, at the end of the day mothers and fathers were still there.

In most cases, it was not until the child had reached their late teens or early to mid-twenties that changes for the better began to take place. It seemed that the continued love of parents had somehow got through to the children. They stopped doubting that they were unwanted or unlovable. Once this point had been reached, it was not unusual for parents and children to become closer than might normally be the case between parents and their grown-up children. It was as if the children were recovering some of the lost intimacy that goes with feeling secure and safe in a relationship. Twenty-five-year-old daughters would begin to phone home several times a week. A son would insist on spoiling his parents, treating them extravagantly at birthdays and anniversaries.

But "sticking with" and "standing by" such children when they were at their very worst was an extremely difficult thing to do. It required putting up with many years of hostility, tension, heartache and pain. Parents needed good, strong support throughout this difficult period. Such support, if it existed, came from partners, friends, professional helpers, the church or having some religious faith.

Some experienced parents who had both born and adopted children maintained full confidence in their parenting skills, even under pressure. Their children's difficulties posed no fundamental threat to their parental abilities. These parents placed no particular expectations on the children and they were not unduly put out or undermined if their children lied or stole. Misbehaviours were recognised and dealt with firmly and fairly. Many adopters, either through instinct or experience, were able to put themselves in their children's shoes and sense their insecurity and anger. This meant that they were less prone to feel irritated, let down or incompetent.

In many cases, though, it was usually the case that either the child left home at a youngish age or the parents were simply no longer able to cope with them being at home and insisted that they leave. These extreme measures became necessary in order to preserve marriages, save families and prevent breakdowns. In this way, parents could offer love, albeit at a distance, instead of feeling lost in the mounting despair, anger and exasperation that was characterising home life.

We now listen to what the parents of these children had to say in more detail. Their stories followed a common pattern. From bad starts through troubled childhoods to angry adolescence, adopters reflected on a history of difficult experiences. However, parents whose children had reached late adolescence or early adulthood were often able to report, if not a completely happy ending, then at least the signs of a more satisfactory and satisfying outcome. If parents had managed to reach this point, their hopes and optimism rose, though always tempered by notes of caution.

These children arrived in one of two ways: some who were placed as young babies got off to a poor start with their adopters, and some joined families as toddlers or older children after suffering a period of either inadequate or incompetent care by one or both of their birth parents. This second group ended up in either foster care or residential care before being placed for adoption.

Babies and bad starts
All the children in this sub-group were placed with their adoptive parents when they were young babies aged somewhere between two and eight weeks. But in spite of their very young age at placement, these babies never developed a confident, relaxed relationship with their carers. They seemed both insecure and irritable, demanding and hyperactive, inconsolable and restless. The word used most often by parents to describe these children, even when they were talking about them as babies, was "angry".

Although a few parents did say that as babies their children were "easy", the majority felt that for a variety of reasons their relationship with their children got off to a bad start. There was no obvious reason why they should run into difficulties so early on. Some adopters whose children developed these angry and hostile patterns were either first time parents or, just as likely, they already had children, whether born or adopted. We have already noted that some parents felt that their children were particularly bright, artistic and sensitive. It may be that such children were peculiarly aware of and susceptible to radical changes and upsets in the quality of their early care. Temperamentally difficult babies, anxious parenting and disturbing pre-placement experiences could all have played a part in bringing about unsettled childhoods. Eileen describes Luke thus:

'Luke was a very difficult baby from the day he arrived. He was highly demanding. He woke up every night until he was three – some nights it would be ten or eleven times a night. He was never satisfied. He could never amuse himself. He demanded your whole attention the whole time. This constant demand for attention interfered with my bonding with him completely. I couldn't bond with him. I felt guilty because I felt I should be loving him. It got so that I wasn't very keen on Luke and he sensed this. He'd squirm if I tried to hold him. I got very little pleasure from him at that time. He was a child who drained you of everything without giving anything back.'

Some mothers felt that their difficulties were self-inflicted and might have been avoided. Oliver was three months old when he was placed with Elaine. He had been with a foster mother. 'He was a big baby; very overweight. I was immediately told to diet this baby,' said Elaine, 'but looking back this was bad advice. It affected our relationship. Not feeding your baby is against all your instincts as a mother. It was too big and depriving a change for Oliver. So in addition to all the other moves and changes I also had to hit him in the gut and he would cry so.' Throughout his childhood, Oliver 'was greedy – he couldn't seem to control his appetite. If he was given a box of chocolates for his birthday, he would eat them all in a day.'

Older children: backgrounds and beginnings

The second sub-group of children who, according to their adopters, became "angry" were those placed after the age of six to twelve months, often as toddlers or pre-school children. They had experienced incompetent parenting prior to their adoption as well as many changes of caretaker during their first few months and years of life. Many had enjoyed some love and attention, but these good times were erratic, unpredictable and usually short-lived. The continued inability of birth mothers to provide care which was consistent led to the children's eventual admission into formal care before finally being placed for adoption. Although not all the children were difficult in their pre-school years, most parents experienced some problems from the outset. Their children were often tetchy or awkward, or they were socially abrasive in dealing with other children and adults. The combination of being both anxious and demanding characterised all of these children. They found it difficult to cope with change and disruption. Anger and anxiety surfaced at the prospect of any separation, say at bed-time or when starting nursery.

The feeling that their children were very strong willed appeared particularly pronounced during toddlerhood. 'When Sadie was a toddler,' remembered Gaye, 'she would sit and have tantrums anywhere. We were once in the middle of Prague and she had one of her tempers. In the hotel she would run away. Totally fearless. Shear grittiness and a very determined little girl. It was when she was this age that I gave birth to Simon. And he and I became incredibly close which was very hard on Sadie. She has had very, very jealous times, poor kid. But she's never been close, never very demonstrative. As a little girl she seemed either very, very happy or almost manic and absolutely bloody awful.'

Ruth

Peter and Catherine were told that Ruth was 'a healthy, white toddler who was bright, alert and responsive.' At that point childless, they thought this was a very positive description, and so decided to go ahead with the adoption. 'We knew the background was a bit grizzly,' said Catherine, 'but the positives seemed to outweigh the negatives.' The birth mother was described as immature. Both the mother and birth father were drug users. They stole credit cards to pay for their habit. When Ruth was six months old, her mother was imprisoned and Ruth was placed with foster carers. Three months later, the mother was released. Ruth returned to her but was sometimes looked after by her parents and sometimes she was left with friends. Many nights, Ruth was left alone at home by her mother. Allegations of neglect mounted. By the time she was eighteen months old, Ruth had been looked after by six different carers.

When she joined Peter and Catherine, she seemed to behave well beyond her two years. 'She strutted about like a little party queen,' recalled Catherine. 'She came up and sat on our laps. Very chatty. I remember thinking at the time "My goodness! This is a bit eerie." It was just surface charm. Just winning some attention from anyone and it didn't matter who. But she did look beautiful and we thought how lucky we were.'

From the beginning, food was very important to Ruth. 'More, more, more all the time.' Catherine invested a great deal of time and affection in Ruth 'but she merely responded in a dead-pan manner. For the first few years she was extremely compliant and helpful. 'But,' added Catherine, 'she never wanted kisses or cuddles, though she thawed a little. If she ever did give you a kiss, it was flat and expressionless.' It also appeared that Ruth was reluctant to give way to her feelings. For example, when she hurt herself, she would try not to cry. 'I well remember the first time Ruth fell over on a concrete path,' said Catherine. 'She really hurt herself and I could see the tears in her eyes, but she just refused to let herself cry.'

Not very good with other people
Throughout most of their childhoods, these children had few close or regular friends. Some children behaved aggressively, even viciously, when they were playing with age-mates. Not surprisingly, they were not always popular. They seemed to lack empathy and social competence. At nursery, one of the staff said to Ruth's mother, 'She will be much better when she can learn to tolerate other people. Ruth prefers playing on her

own.' She had no friends as a girl. Between the ages of seven and twelve, 'Ruth was insufferable with other children,' said her mother. 'She bullied them, dominated them. She had a vicious tongue. She would pinch, kick, steal. We'd get complaints from their parents about her behaviour in the playground.'

School

None of the children, whether adopted as babies or older, had a trouble-free time at school. Teachers would say that they lacked concentration or were socially disruptive in the classroom. It was not unusual for some children to avoid testing situations. 'He was extremely adept at avoiding exams or any competitive situation. He considered himself a failure. He couldn't listen and he couldn't concentrate.' Academic achievements were poor or disappointing. The children's absorption with emotional issues seemed to push any thoughts of academic success out of their minds. The more pressured the school environment, the less well these children coped. Truancy and school refusal would increase during adolescence. In the more serious cases, teenage children would miss months or even years of school. And in spite of the alleged high intelligence of this group, most either avoided being assessed or performed badly in exams. Progression on to higher education was very much the exception rather than the rule.

Poor concentration and 'a lack of sticking power' was a common failing. Parents dreaded school open evenings: 'We always spent hours on Eric,' said Pru, 'and hardly any time on the others. They would say things like "Eric is very artistic and creative but in everything he is underachieving." He expected to be criticised all the time. He was wilfully slow getting ready for school in the mornings and he made me feel so negative towards him because he kept making my life so bloody difficult.'

Adam

Adam's behaviour went steadily downhill from the day he started to the day he was finally expelled. Lucy described a catalogue of worsening events. She described him as 'a beautiful looking boy'. At first she could not believe that Adam could possibly be doing anything wrong. One teacher said that Adam was devious and would tell you any story in order to get his own way.

'But then he got worse at school. He would lock himself in the toilets and wouldn't come out. The teachers couldn't bear Adam. He would climb on the school roof. The others boys would turn on him . . . He heaved a brick through a window and said he did it for a dare. He stole some gloves. Throughout his prep school we were always getting phone calls about him. He ran away three times. I got to dread the phone. It was a good school and the headmaster was very patient. He then went on to public school which was a total and complete disaster. He made no sustained friendships. The teachers didn't like him. Then the phone calls started coming again. He'd set alight to the dormitory "by mistake". He lost interest in everything. He associated with the worst boys in the school. He became very devious. He began truanting. No work whatsoever. . . When he was fifteen, we brought him home and tried him at the local public school as a day pupil. We then had three solid years of trauma. He would lie. He would truant. The teachers gave up on him. He would disappear and go missing all night. He seemed so unhappy and hated everything and by this time we were losing control of him completely.'

Most of the children from a minority ethnic background experienced racism at school. Children who fell into the "angry" pattern and who were from a minority ethnic background were therefore having to cope with a range of emotional and social difficulties at school. Teachers were not always sensitive to these issues. As she talked about Oliver's school career, Elaine described some of the racism with which her son routinely had to cope:

'By the time he was eight. I was forever being called up to the school for one thing and another. He was always being told off for fighting in the playground. And we are talking about a child who was as gentle as gentle could be with animals and babies. And once, while we were waiting to see the teacher he whispered to me: "They call me shit. They call me names because of my colour." So I would encourage Oliver to tell the teacher. But all she said was, "Oh well, names are not very important." She just dismissed it totally. I told her it was desperately important for Oliver and very hurtful for a little boy of eight but she seemed to have no idea.

For all the children described as "angry", school life and choice of friends went very much together. Parents rarely felt that their children made a wise choice of friends. There were three kinds of worry. The majority of the children either made no close friends or were not liked by their peers. Secondly, there were children who had not coped well socially; they showed off and were attention-seeking. And thirdly, many children had associated with others who, like themselves, were disruptive, unruly or even criminal.

Adolescence: lying, stealing and other bad behaviour
One of the key characteristics of these children was that their initial anger was clearly directed at their parents. Mothers in particular were on the receiving end of a lot of confused hostility. Constant lying and denial meant that parents no longer believed a word their children said. Nearly all the children went through a phase, often lasting many years, of very anti-social behaviour.

Although most children had been "difficult" since the day they arrived, a few had not been regarded as particularly problematic by their parents until the onset of adolescence when, suddenly, their behaviour deteriorated. But whether gradual or sudden, the degree of misbehaviour exhibited in adolescence could be quite alarming. Violence as well as criminal behaviour was common. The aggression and hostility, initially aimed at parents, would then spill beyond family life into school and the local community. Thefts from home would be followed by more serious offences outside the home. At home, many parents who had money or cheque books taken, developed a siege mentality. Handbags, purses and wallets would be carried at all times. Doors to areas of the house where there were valuables were heavily locked. Larders and fridges would be raided for food, though some children were refusing to eat with the rest of the family. Home life came under great strain as old and relaxed habits had to be swapped for new, stricter, tighter and more cautious regimes.

Mothers and fathers found themselves involved with agencies and authorities which they could scarcely have imagined a few years earlier. Education welfare officers, social workers, police officers and educational psychologists became familiar figures in some households.

At this time, relationships between parents and children often reached breaking point. Some children refused to take part in home life. Parents and family life were "rubbished" by the children. They insisted on eating their meals at separate times; they took food from the fridge which would be hoarded in their bedrooms. Some of the children who were more emotionally disturbed cut themselves. Girls began sexual relationships at an early age and a number found themselves pregnant. Abortions or early parenthood followed.

Marriages were put under strain. Schools found it increasingly difficult to cope with the disruptiveness. A couple of boys developed a frightening interest in weapons. They would hide them under pillows or in drawers. In his mid teens, Andrew began to talk about killing his mother. 'He told his school he was frightened that he might kill me,' said Wendy, 'and that was why he didn't want to go home.' Running away or staying out all night worried and exhausted parents. Complaints from teachers, neighbours and the police increased. In their darkest moments, some children said that they felt they did not belong; they felt rejected.

The cumulative effect on parents of so much disruption and disturbance made them feel like giving up. 'It was a nightmare period,' said Roger's mother. When the children were away, parents felt great relief, though levels of guilt and despair rose. Professional support was desperately sought, but the help received was usually disappointing and ineffective, though there were some notable exceptions from post-adoption specialists.

Perversely, the emotional significance of parents for these children meant that mothers and fathers were on the receiving end of their confusion, anger and hostility. It seemed to the parents that their children's demands could never be satisfied. To give and give without receiving any thanks or seeing any improvement was deeply dispiriting and for many parents, their emotional well eventually ran dry. The following story provides a more detailed account of one "angry" child's entry into adolescence.

Eva

As a baby, Eva was repeatedly neglected. She was several times found undernourished. Her birth mother was young and incompetent, her birth father was violent and unstable. She experienced a number of episodes in care, including an attempt at long-term fostering which broke down when Eva was three years old. 'The foster father said: "Either she goes or I do."' She was then placed for adoption with Celia and her husband, a white child with a white couple. 'She was very inquisitive. As soon as she arrived she started looking through all my bags. She wasn't the least bit shy. In those early days, we'd have lots of temper tantrums and screams if she couldn't get her own way. She mutilated all her toys. She'd twist off the arms and legs of all her dolls.'

Although she liked school the teachers found her a "pest". Her ability to concentrate was poor. Nobody could tell her how to do something: 'I know how to do that. You don't need to tell me.' Her teacher commented: 'She said she didn't need to learn joined up writing because she could write fast enough with ordinary writing. She didn't want to do colouring because she wasn't going to be an artist.' Eva was noisy and wanted to interfere all the time. 'The other children were not too tolerant of her because she liked to nip and push and pull them. She never had a best friend although she was always with somebody.' This was how Celia described Eva at the age of ten:

'She seemed to be two completely different kinds of people. This is what I wrote about her at the time. "She's two different people. One – she's outgoing, friendly, helpful, loving, generous, talkative, sensible, forgiving, organising and intelligent. The other – she's mythering, argumentative, bossy, irritating, quarrelsome, insensitive, tormenting, tantrum-throwing, childish, unpleasant, awkward, offensive, untruthful and dishonest." She could switch between the two. And as she got older, she got more devious. She could lie off the top of her head. She seemed to believe what she was saying. She started stealing money from my purse, so I had to get much more careful. Money ran through her fingers like water. She had to spend it if she got hold of any. And she could lose her temper.

She once smashed a full-length mirror in her bedroom because she was annoyed at something about her appearance.'

When Eva was fifteen, Celia felt she was losing control:
'Eva lied a great deal. The school phoned me up to say they had caught her smoking. Eva categorically denied this. They also said they had found her crying copiously, but again she totally denied it. I said to her "Would you confide in me, Eva?" "No," she said, "I'd never confide in any adult. And you nag me too much. You're too strict with me. You won't let me go anywhere." At that stage I wasn't taking any of this that seriously. I laughed at her and said "Oh, that's what mums do. Unfortunately you're my daughter and I've got to tell you." She then ran out and obviously had taken the word "unfortunately" the wrong way, thinking I meant "unfortunately you are my daughter".'

A few months later, the relationship between Celia and Eva suddenly broke down. After a row and a misunderstanding, Eva stormed out of the house but returned a short while later. Upon her return, Celia seemed to see Eva in a new light:
'And then suddenly, I looked at Eva. I thought Oh my god! There's somebody in there I don't know. It was a cold, hard person I'd never seen before. I felt she could have stabbed me in the back and never felt a thing. And that frightened me. And at that point, I burst into tears. "Eva," I said, "have you any idea how I feel?" "No," she said, "why should I care? Don't cry mum. Don't make me try to feel guilty. I haven't done anything wrong." And at that point I said "Oh go away!" meaning from the room. And within minutes, she must have gone. She disappeared. We couldn't find her. We tried friends, the police. The next day, we got a visit from a social worker. Eva was refusing to come home. She said she would see her Dad, but when he got to the children's centre, she locked herself in the toilet and refused to see him. We were all so distraught. She had said I hated her and had thrown her out.'

Eva was taken to a social services assessment centre. For the first three months she would not speak to her mother, only her father. At Christmas, Eva bought presents for her sister and father, but not her mother. Eva then agreed to see Celia, but when her mother went to the centre, Eva refused to meet her. During her stay at the centre, Eva took drugs, she self-mutilated by scratching her face and wrists with a picture hook, and suffered a short episode of anorexia. On one occasion she set fire to a room in the centre. As a result, the staff placed her in a secure unit. At the time of the interview, Eva was sixteen and had been at the centre for eight months. She was still very angry with her mother and could not understand why Celia did not come and "rescue" her from the secure unit: 'You could have objected to me being here. Why didn't you come and get me out?' Celia reflected ruefully:

'Looking back, maybe her greed was in fact her need – her need for things and her need to be loved, I don't know. I can see that she can never really have trusted me. She's wanted to be the boss and dominate me to the point where I felt totally imprisoned. She wouldn't leave me alone. She seemed to want to own me. When it all suddenly broke down, it was such a shock. We both nearly had nervous breakdowns. The social workers made us feel very guilty. She didn't seem to have a conscience about lying or being dishonest. I guess she must have thought that me seeming to reject her was no different to her first mother rejecting her. At the weekend, she said she was going to kill herself if she had to stay in the centre any longer. She asked to come home. But I can't take her at the moment. I couldn't sleep easy in my bed at nights.'

Being adopted: anger and ambivalence

At the heart of the "angry" child's behaviour and development seemed to be a deep uncertainty and ambivalence about adoption and what it meant. This was generally expressed as anger and hostility towards parents, although it could also easily spill over onto brothers and sisters and relationships in general. For example, Andrew had always claimed that he did not want to talk about his adoption. He vehemently said that he was not interested in his background. 'But one day when I was clearing out his room,' said his mother, 'I found all his adoption papers carefully hidden at the back of one of his drawers. He must have removed them from our file.'

The children seemed troubled, hurt and angry that they had been given up for adoption. The adoption appeared to indicate rejection, and rejection suggested that they were unwanted and unloved. And to be unwanted and unloved meant that they were unworthy and unlovable.

The feelings generated by the swirl of such barely conscious thoughts were difficult as well as troubling. A deep emotional ambivalence pervaded all close relationships. They seemed angry with their birth mothers for giving them up and their adopters for taking them away and accepting them. It was their adoptive mother's and father's very existence which seemed to act as a constant reminder to the children that their's was a relationship born out of the original rejection and loss. As Ruth said to her adoptive mother, 'I could understand my mother not coping on her own, but what I cannot see and what I shall never forgive is that when she did have a chance of settling down with this new man, she chose the man and not me.' These proved to be very, very hard thoughts to digest for these children.

These confused and annoying thoughts and feelings rumbled throughout their childhoods, but they became more clearly defined and directed during adolescence. It was then that relationships between parents and children took a steep tumble. The ambivalence expressed itself in rather puzzling and contradictory behaviour. Children were angry and hostile towards the parents and yet they were reluctant to leave them or ignore them. They were preoccupied with the very people against whom they expressed their anger. The result was a nagging, rude presence that did not seem to want or be able to go away. It was rather like the young child who has a fierce temper tantrum who keeps following the parent around even as he or she gets more and more angry with that parent. Parents felt that they could not win in these situations. If they stayed and tried to talk with their children, the anger, abuse and hostility mounted. If they attempted to leave or give up on the relationship, the children felt rejected, desperate and angry. In spite of the anger and hostility, these were anxious and vulnerable children, sensitive to criticism and afraid of failure.

For the adopters, this was a very confusing and exhausting recipe.

Basic instincts and love for the children would keep them going for several years. A heavy price was sometimes paid for staying with these desperate but endlessly demanding children. Marriages came under strain. Brothers and sisters felt confused and neglected as their demanding sibling seemed to dominate family life.

It seemed that for these children, parental giving – whether of love, attention, money, food – was somehow equated with being loved and wanted and yet such giving could never quite be trusted, which is why the demands never seemed to stop. As the children wore down their parents, it seemed that their feared unlovability and unworthiness were, in fact, true. Many mothers and fathers eventually gave in and gave up. Seventeen-year-olds were asked to leave. Life at home seemed to be so full of conflict and tension that the only way to recover anything like a normal life was to insist that the children moved out. There was a terrible and sad self-fulfilling quality in these parent–child relationships. The children's deep fears, anger and insecurities brought about a repeat of the parental rejection that led to their adoption in the first place.

Most children, though, stopped being quite so angry sometime in their late teens or early twenties. It was as if they could finally begin to trust and accept the unconditional love of their parents. They experienced the beginnings of feeling secure. Their feelings of self-worth improved. But reaching this stage could be a long, tiring haul. Parents felt, as one mother phrased it, 'put through the wringer'.

Morag, an adoptive mother, relayed the following incident in an attempt to explain her daughter Imogen's immaturity, confusion and hurt:

'When she was eighteen, we came home one evening and found her and some of her friends drunk. She went bananas and stayed out in the garden until three in the morning. She snapped one of the young trees. And then she did the very same thing the following weekend! I couldn't believe it. I followed her out into the garden saying – I know it sounds rather pathetic – "There, there. It's all right." And she was pouring all this stuff out about me saying that I should never have had children, that I was useless, and how she couldn't talk to me. And then she muttered some kind of witches curse on me about how not only should I not have had her but that I wasn't ever going to see any grandchildren. She'd really thought it through. And then she went back into the house wailing and rolling about breaking things. It was tragic really. And we kept saying through all this "We love you". We can have good days together – we went to the theatre together recently. And then something ghastly happens. It's as if she can't bear to have things too calm.'

Leaving home
By mid-adolescence, many of the children found being in close relationship with their parents very difficult. It was as if they wanted to be loved but simply could not trust the genuineness or permanency of that love. These were desperate children who had no idea how to cope with loving relationships. If the ambivalence could not be resolved, one way out of the tension was to leave home. This was accomplished or precipitated in a number of ways. As part of the build up in tension, children stayed out late all night, went missing for the odd day, or ran away repeatedly. If schools and parents could not cope, children might be sent away to live in a boarding school. The schools were either in the private sector or residential units run by the local authority for children who are emotionally and behaviourally disturbed.

Some children seemed more at ease with the structures and routines of institutional care. Others left home as soon as they had finished their schooling. They tried living in bedsits or with friends. But friends soon ran out of patience and asked them to leave. A period of being unsettled and rootless followed.

Twenty and beyond: the calm after the storm
In most cases, the anger and hostility of these preoccupied and agitated children seemed finally to blow themselves out. The age at which this happened varied. In some cases a calmer mood would descend by the time they had reached seventeen or eighteen while in others it could be as late as twenty seven or twenty eight.

If parents managed to "stay with" their "angry" son or daughter through adolescence and beyond, often they experienced not only a more relaxed relationship, but in some instances a particularly affectionate one. It was as if the now grown-up child had finally accepted, at a barely conscious level, that they really were loved and wanted. Their anger was exhausted. They could start to bond and attach with their parents, albeit fifteen to twenty odd years after their arrival. This accounted for some of the increased contact, interest and concern that began to characterise many parent–child relationships in this late stage. Frequent contact, choosing to live nearby, and the buying of generous presents were not unusual. All of this came as a great relief and a pleasant surprise to parents.

But this happy if somewhat unexpected outcome did not happen in every case. For those parents who said that their 'lives had been made hell' and whose only way out seemed to be to ask their child to leave, the broken contact was not always easy to mend. Many years might pass without any communication. Even so, the parents often learned that the once-so-difficult and angry child was now 'settled' or 'happily married with two children' or 'doing well'. And even in the cases in which contact had been resumed and relationships were good, it was not uncommon for a parent to conclude 'We get on fine now – so long as we don't have to live under the same roof together though!'

Rod

For some children, one of the contributory factors in defusing the anger was when they sought information about, and in some cases made contact with, their birth parents. When Rod was nearly eighteen, Greta was quite keen that he looked for his birth mother but he was reluctant. However, he allowed his mother to make some enquiries, and on his eighteenth birthday he received a birthday card, a letter and a photograph from his birth mother. 'He was over the moon,' recalls Greta, and he wrote a 'lovely letter' back to her. However, she had never told her children of his existence. Rod's father was African-Caribbean. His white mother had finally married a white man. 'I got quite angry with her. She did not want to meet Rod. And writing to him had cost her nothing.'

Rod then managed to trace his birth father via the electoral roll in Birmingham. 'It turns out,' says Greta, 'that his dad's family had been thinking about him for all those eighteen years. They had never wanted to give him up. Their reaction compared to his mother's meant that they went up in his estimation. The family welcomed him. His paternal grandmother told him she had prayed for him every single day. And it meant so much to Rod. They're now his family as well as us. My husband and I divorced some years ago. So I'm Rod's mother and Roy – his birth father – is his Dad as far as Rod is concerned. Rod is training and working in catering. He lives away from home and has a girlfriend – which is funny because when he was young he used to say "I wouldn't want girlfriends. I wouldn't like them to get hurt when I wanted to break it off and had to leave." Isn't that interesting?'

There were hints that although relationships between grown-up children and parents generally improved, many adopted adults remained emotionally a little fragile and vulnerable. Jobs were secured and maintained, but dealings with other people were sometimes less stable. As adults and as adolescents, some children in this group continued to feel that the world was often against them. Setbacks and upsets were always seen as the fault of other people.

Harriett

After Val had given birth to Philip, she suffered secondary infertility. A few years later she adopted Harriett who remained convinced that Philip was the preferred child. 'She always seemed so insecure,' said Val. In her mid-teens, Harriett had stolen money from her parents and shoplifted. 'She seemed to resent us having her.'

Harriett and her brother Philip did not get on. Not longer after Harriett had moved house, she came to visit her parents but found only Philip at home. 'For whatever reason, they ended up having an almighty row which we walked in to. She started screaming at us that we preferred Philip, that I had given birth to him. There was a lot of pent-up emotion, mainly directed at me,' said Val.

'We didn't see her then for four years. In the interim periods we met some friends who said "Has Harriett had her baby yet?" And we said, "Baby? What baby?" "You did know that she is married?" But of course, we didn't. She had married Len six months earlier. We felt dreadful. But we never closed the door on her. We always sent her birthday cards and Christmas cards . . .

'Unthinkingly, when she was pregnant, I had things of hers that had come with her when she was a baby, and rightly or wrongly, probably wrongly, I packed them up and sent them to her with a little note saying perhaps she would like to have them for her baby. They came back through the post with obscenities written on the outside of the parcel in inch high letters saying she didn't want any memorabilia, and her child was going to have a happy childhood and all this sort of thing. We were very upset . . . I feel that looking back that she was a very angry young woman; a very insecure young woman. And maybe somewhere along the line, I don't where, we failed her . . .

'Just over a year later we were on holiday. I had not seen Harriett for several years. But I sent her a postcard and put on the bottom "Happy birthday to your little girl. I think she must be about one now." You see I didn't even know when her birthday was. "I expect she's lovely. You were at that age. Bring her over to see us sometime." Two months later the phone rang and a cheerful voice at the other end of the line said, "Hello. It's Harriett here. Are you in this morning? Can I bring Emily over to meet you?" Just like that! I said, "Of course you can." Half an hour later she was over. I was in tears by the time she arrived. She now comes over most weeks. She has another baby. Len, her husband, has a good job, but has admitted to me that he does have difficulties with her sometimes. He once said, "You don't have to live with her!" And I said, "Oh yes we did. For eighteen years, Len!" She's on the phone to me nearly every day. She's so utterly different. She's a changed person. She still likes her own way and seeks attention. But we have a good relationship . . .

'In 1991, she traced her birth mother. I didn't hear much about it, but I've now been told that she's supposed to have died in a car crash. I don't know if it's true. It could be just a way of saying "I don't care for her". She's sort of killed her off.

'Looking back over the last thirty odd years, at one stage we thought maybe we should never have adopted because we felt so desperate. Whatever we did with her, we were rebuffed. But it now seems that now she's got her own family and children she seems to understand. I couldn't ask for a better relationship with her now. We bent over backwards to treat her and Philip the same, but she never saw it that way. It never felt that way to her. Deep down, I'm sure she was tremendously insecure.'

Wiser and humbler

The following story is given in more detail. Although there was much turbulence, calmer waters were eventually reached by the time Amy reached her mid-twenties. But along the way, her parents felt they had learned so much about life that they felt vastly wiser as well as much, much humbler. They had no doubt that the lessons had been learned the hard way, but they felt that dealing with a child with such demanding and disturbed behaviour had made them better human beings.

Amy

Placed at five weeks old, Amy was Marjorie's first child. From the moment she arrived, Amy was 'either being terrible or wonderful'. The adoption worker visited regularly during the first few months but only succeeded in unsettling Marjorie and making her feel more anxious about her fitness to be a mother. There was a moment when Marjorie felt very depressed: 'I suppose it was wanting a baby for so long and I can remember sitting one day for some extraordinary reason feeling completely depressed. I didn't understand why.' Things were made worse when there was a hiccup over the birth mother signing the adoption papers. 'I thought she might want Amy back. I even planned how I would escape with her and go round the world and stay with different friends so that I could keep her.'

Even as a baby 'Amy would have temper tantrums that would last for ages. And as a toddler she would have screaming fits that lasted an hour.' Marjorie said that the temper tantrums were like 'thunderstorms – violent while they were happening but calm afterwards'. At one stage Marjorie even wondered if Amy might be autistic: 'She was so clever and responsive and yet so difficult.'

When she started school, Amy refused to go. She undressed herself just before they were about to start out in the mornings. She would not eat at set times; she would only wear what she wanted, even if it was a summer's dress on a cold winter's day: 'She was totally her own person.' Marjorie felt confused about how to handle Amy. She took her to a child psychiatrist 'but he was no use at all – cold and intellectual – making me feel I wasn't doing anything right.'

Amy managed to gain a place in a high ability school, but the teachers found her very difficult. She would not do the work and she wanted her own way all the time. And at home, too, she continued to be demanding. 'There were so many arguments,' recalled Marjorie, 'and she was so intolerant. Amy would get terribly upset if a point was misinterpreted. Justice had to be absolutely, exactly right. There wasn't any room for manoeuvre; there were no grey areas.' Every evening, Marjorie and her husband Cameron would have 'an inquest' on the day's events. They would wonder where they were going wrong.

Her junior school refused to let her progress to its senior school. Marjorie and Cameron made the decision to send Amy, aged eleven, to boarding school. But again, the teachers did not find Amy easy and there were threats to expel her. 'She led the staff a merry dance. It was as if Amy had had bad and good in her in equal parts and they were fighting each other. She got involved with some other difficult girls. She started smoking and by seventeen she was into drugs.'

Marjorie described incidents when Amy appeared angry and confused about her adoption. One day, when she was nine years old, she said out of the blue 'I want to go back'. For most of the time, Amy did not want to know anything about her adoption. 'She would say "She gave me away, so I'm not interested. She didn't want me, so I don't want her!" It was a fierce reaction. And at the same time she would be sort of saying to me "And anyway, who do you think you are to take over my parenting? You're not my mother, so I don't want you either." So she became a victim even though she's been surrounded by love.'

Amy had managed to pass a reasonable number of her 'O' level exams but never managed to complete her 'A' levels. The drug scene took over. She left school and helped out in a shop. There were nights when she did not return home. Eventually, Amy was allowed to live in the flat that went with the shop. Just before her nineteenth birthday, Amy told her mother that she was pregnant. She decided to have an abortion and almost immediately afterwards 'had a sort of mental breakdown. She was drugging with all her dreadful friends. It was a nightmare.'

Amy returned home and began to self-abuse. She would cut her arms. It was at this time she got involved with a man who stole and committed burglaries. The police caught him and he was sent to prison. Marjorie then helped Amy find a flat of her own. By now Marjorie was tired but found herself becoming increasingly reflective and philosophical. 'Your sights and your standards change all the time. You only want them to be happy. You keep revising what you'll settle for. So I settled for her living with this awful man in a flat. When he came out of prison, he painted all the windows black and had all his druggy friends in. The flat was absolutely destroyed. He beat her up.'

Amy and her boyfriend found themselves in ever more serious trouble. Matters came to a head when they stole a credit card and bought hundreds of pounds worth of clothes and drink. Amy was arrested and taken to prison. Her heroin addiction was recognised and she was sent for treatment in a special clinic. Upon release she found a new boyfriend whom she soon married. Although the marriage lasted a number of years, Amy's husband drank, took drugs and was violent towards her. In her mid-twenties, Amy was raped and this precipitated her return to drugs. Marjorie accepted her back home but events took one more turn for the worse:

'One evening I came home. Cameron was out. There was blood all over the kitchen and I thought he must have defrosted some meat. Careless man, I thought. I then went upstairs. Amy was sitting bleeding everywhere and drugged. It was a horrible moment. She had tried suicide on a number of occasions . . . Anyway, after that incident I bought her a car and encouraged her to start a mobile hairdressing business. She had always been very artistic. Very creative. I was indulgent still. I was so naïve. Of course, it simply made it easier for her to run around dealing in drugs. So, they caught her eventually with 30 grams of heroin and again took her off to prison. I visited her in prison. It was so horrible to see your child in that situation.'

Amy was bailed to attend a rehabilitation clinic. Her appearance in court resulted in a probation order. Marjorie not only went with her daughter to court but spoke on her behalf. Two days before the case was heard, Amy married another "junkie".

'By that time I felt absolutely empty. It was then that I decided that we had to find her birth mother. It might help. Cameron and I dug out Amy's file and papers . . . By Monday of the following week we had a phone call from Amy's birth mother's husband. I'd been thinking about Amy's birth mother for nearly thirty years. You can't have a baby without thinking about her mother . . . You can't really not think about her. You're grateful to them and you worry about them. This lady then came to the phone. I couldn't believe it!'

Amy's birth mother had married and had more children. She said that she had a 'a lot to digest' but that she would make contact again. Marjorie then told Amy what she had done. 'You've done what?!' said Amy. 'What did you do that for? *You're* my mother.' 'And then she said "Well, if it helps you Mum, it's all right."'

'By now, I thought she had really appreciated that we'd hung in there. There was a time when she had said 'Why do you keep on rescuing me? I'm going to use you and I'm going to use you until you won't let me use you any longer.' She said that to me in one of her drug states. But I didn't give up because I love her. She's so intelligent, she's so vulnerable and I somehow feel that she has this self-destruction streak in her. I want to protect her. I want her to be happy.'

Marjorie and Cameron had a successful meeting with Amy's birth mother and husband. The birth mother was intelligent, successful and "posh". In due course, Amy met her birth mother. Their reunion was successful and continues. 'We're all still in contact,' said Marjorie. 'Amy still sees me as her mother. But since meeting her birth mother, our relationship is better. Amy is still very itchy and scratchy if she senses criticism.' She is about to be divorced from her second husband. She hopes to start Art college. Reflecting on the present and the past, Marjorie summed up the last thirty years, saying:

'I'm optimistic now. I think everything will be fine. Amy has taken me to places and led me down corridors of pain and joy and hope that I didn't know existed . . . You can't go through life and have experiences like that without being changed. I think life is a great leveller.'

Looking back

There was no doubting that for all parents, these "angry" children had been very wearing. Looking back, there were a range of views. For those still in the throes of difficult and hostile relationships with their children, the feelings about the adoption were negative. Parents who had weathered the storm and were beginning to enjoy calmer times offered a more philosophical outlook. They did not deny the trauma of the adolescent years but were pleased they had 'stuck with' their son or daughter. Their lives had been changed by their experiences, making them more modest and tolerant human beings. A third group viewed their adoption of these difficult children as a worthwhile and rewarding achievement. They had few expectations of these very emotionally and behaviourally damaged children and were not surprised or too devastated by their worst excesses. They gave without expecting anything in return. Every little positive step was viewed as a huge bonus. Their philosophy was that every child needs a home, and that something is always better than nothing when it comes to good social relationships. Although their children did misbehave and did go through periods of surliness and anger, on the whole they did not become as forlorn, hostile and violent as many of the other children described in this group.

Parents who viewed the adoption with either ambivalence or regret said they had experienced little pleasure in raising such difficult children. 'Knowing what I know now,' sighed Greta, 'I wouldn't adopt again.' Adolescence was generally regarded as the most distressing time. Tensions ran high and marriages came under considerable strain. Brothers and sisters, especially if they were the only other child in the house, often suffered. In these cases, parents found it hard to forgive their son or daughter for almost ruining their sibling's childhood. Tiredness and guilt tinged with relief followed a long and traumatic episode.

Some parents felt very philosophical about the difficult times that they had with their children. 'I must say this about it all,' said Leisha's father, 'it took me into spheres of life that I did not expect to experience. Police stations, courts, prisons, psychiatrists, lawyers . . . But experiences are part of life and perhaps my philosophy is that such experiences enlarge you in some sort of sense.'

Experienced parents, parents with birth and adopted children, and parents who had fostered as well as raised their own children seemed most able to review their "angry" children with a warm, forgiving eye. 'The kind of rewards element that everyone needs is virtually non-existent in these children,' said Marilyn. 'You have to see it in a different way. I have had my own kids and that has fulfilled me and met all those kinds of needs. With the more difficult children, it's very rewarding, just to see, that the fact we only have one life, and that in spite of rotten beginnings people end up OK.'

Peggy, who, over a number of years, had adopted five young children whose behaviour was difficult and disturbed, had no doubts about the rewards:

'Seeing these children advance . . . I mean, there's times when you have problems and I find the stealing and the lying very difficult. But when you look at these children and think back to when they came and how damaged they were, and you look at them now – that's my reward! True, I've had sleepless nights crying about and worrying over them. I've wept buckets, for example, when Lara wouldn't let me get close to her for years. But I think if you take children for what they are and not for what you want them to be, and enjoy them for themselves, then that's what they want. They want to be wanted.'

9   Uninvolved and wary children

Children who experienced *rejection* and *many changes of caretaker* during their first few years of life behaved in one of two ways: either they found it difficult to become fully involved in any new family life, or they were so unused to having close emotional relationships that they treated the members of their adoptive family no differently to most other people. Before being adopted, both sets of children had a history of neglect, physical and sexual abuse and a large number of inconsistent, unreliable relationships with a series of caregivers. Love did not appear to have featured in their lives in this pre-adoption stage. Emotionally, they had had to fend for themselves. Many had been in children's homes for several years. When they eventually arrived to live with their new parents, the adopters, as far the children were concerned, were just the latest in a long line of potentially indifferent or hostile carers.

Throughout their childhoods, these children proved difficult. Much of their behaviour was disturbed. Most received some kind of psychological or psychiatric help, though it was rarely successful. Emotionally, they were often distant and somewhat detached. 'Des's life,' said his mother, 'has been utter chaos. He couldn't look me in the eyes for two years.' It was difficult to get close to them and as they grew older they drifted further away. They would typically leave home early preferring to live alone, either at boarding school, in hostels or flats, or occasionally even sleep rough. Often, girls would leave around sixteen or seventeen, using boyfriends as a vehicle for their exit. Some would have their first baby whilst still in their late teens. However, they found it difficult to form and sustain intimate relationships.

Several parents described their adolescent children as "wanderers". They would disappear from home and go missing for days or even weeks before they surfaced again. The more distant children tried to cope with relationships by cutting off. As teenagers, the children would often say that they felt they did not belong and would drift off, emotionally and even physically. And yet, even though they might have been out of contact for some time, they would reappear for a while, before once again precipitating a quarrel and storming off.

Behaviour could be difficult from the day they arrived, but it would grow worse during adolescence. Lying and stealing put strains on family life. They were children who lacked patience and had low levels of tolerance. Friends were few and many were "loners". Exhausted and very sad, some parents had moments when they felt glad to see them go.

For children placed at an older age, the neglect and disruption they experienced had extended over a long period of time. The older the children, the more memories of mothers and fathers, foster carers and residential carers they had. By the age of four, five and six, these were very emotionally damaged and often quite behaviourally disturbed young people. Emotionally, these children were not easy to reach. Relationships with them would lack reciprocity. They would be impulsive and emotionally uncontrolled.

The more disorganised children, many of whom joined their new families after long spells in children's homes, were indiscriminate about whom they related with. They were restless, unfocused children. Relationships were used mainly to meet needs and gratify desires. 'Take, take, take until we were sucked dry,' was how one mother described her relationship with her daughter. When needs were not met, these children became frustrated, irritable and angry.

Schools did not find them easy to discipline or teach. They would be disorganised and disruptive. Many were removed by the age of nine or ten to special schools or small, private boarding schools. Most left school with few, if any, academic qualifications. They were not very socially skilled children, and a few were described by their adopters as bullies or aggressive. Levels of tolerance, concentration and confidence were low. A few had eating problems – either eating too much or not enough. In adult life, this sometimes led to problems with alcohol.

Adolescence marked a further deterioration of behaviour. Lying, deviousness and manipulative behaviour were described by many mother and fathers. Nearly all the children stole money and other valuables from their parents. The children tended to leave home at a relatively early age, choosing to live on their own or, if their parents could afford it, go to boarding school. Once the children had left home, contact with them would be sporadic and unpredictable. Some parents felt a sense of relief after their children had gone. Although a few children were beginning to lead more settled lives by their mid-twenties, their behaviour continued to suggest both emotional immaturity and insecurity. Relationships were still a problem for many of those in their twenties, though gradual improvements were noted by many parents.

Many children who were placed at a much older age – say nine, ten, eleven – and who had experienced a long history of neglect and rejection followed by several years in a children's home never fully integrated into their new family life. They remained uncommitted. Although their behaviour might not always be as difficult as those with a similar background placed at a younger age, much of their life was led independent of the family. They hovered in and out of being close as if uncertain to trust being intimate. As they got older, these children would "wander in and out" of family life. This hesitancy in committing themselves to family relationships carried on into early adulthood, though in many cases there were very gradual attempts to get closer and more involved. The build up of trust in close relationships was painfully slow for these children. Gradually, very gradually, and if their parents had managed to stay with them, the grown-up children made more and more frequent returns home. It was as if they were still exploring the constancy and reliability of intimate family life.

Background and beginnings

After a history of neglectful or rejecting relationships, the children's behaviour was variously excited and disorganised, indiscriminate and casual. There were odd surprises. Polly, aged five and Neil, aged seven, had spent the previous four years in a children's home. They had never seen their meals being prepared. It just arrived on a plate. 'So,' said Fiona, their adoptive mother, 'when I produced a roast chicken on the table to be carved, Polly said "Oh, look, a great big white fish!"'

Graham and Edna first met Giles, aged two, at a London hospital. 'He'd had the most horrendous start. He'd been totally rejected. He was malnourished and very underweight. He'd been taken into hospital by social workers when he was a baby. They built him up and sent him back to his mother. But within a few months he was back in the hospital again. She never changed him; she didn't feed him. His mother left him in his cot twenty four hours a day. He was fed once a day. He was never lifted or cuddled. He couldn't talk. He couldn't even sit up. When we first saw him, he had these big eyes but no smiles. He couldn't talk or even walk.'

For the first week in his new home, Giles constantly banged his head against his cot, the chair or the door. However, he quickly learned to walk. And as soon as he was mobile 'he just tore around the house'. He reacted to everyone in the same demanding way, whether they were his new parents, their friends or strangers visiting the house.

Instincts helped some parents to deal with their children and their disturbed behaviour. Alice described Kylie's background prior to her arrival, aged four. She had a long history of abuse and neglect. 'Social workers had found her tied to a high chair. She had scabies. Everyone who had looked after her had rejected her. She was fed by her older sister who was barely older than Kylie herself. The only words she uttered when she came were "Kylie naughty – go in cot." She came with the saddest face I have ever seen. She had switched everything off. A dead child.' Alice's second born son, David, then aged fifteen, became involved:

'David would hold Kylie and rock her for hours. He would talk gently with her and get her to respond. He's always been absolutely devoted to Kylie. She was a child who needed an awful lot of love. I decided, even at four, to give her a bottle again. I don't think she'd been a baby ever. She'd never been cuddled or had a bottle to suck. She remained in herself for a long while.'

Holding back and holding on

Although the children initially often settled in well, from the beginning they seemed emotionally a little remote, a little restrained. Not having experienced much in the way of closeness or reliable intimacy, they found it difficult to trust other people. They were wary and nervous of becoming too emotionally involved. They coped by keeping people, including their parents, at a slight emotional distance. At first this was disappointing for mothers and fathers. 'She was never cuddlesome,' or 'She was very self-contained,' were typical observations. Although the emotional detachment was disappointing for most parents while their children were young, they could live with it. However, by adolescence this unrewarding unreachability could turn into a source of irritation.

Andrew, for example, had been badly neglected as a baby. He was found abandoned in a flat when he was six months old. Although he physically thrived in the children's home, emotionally he did not develop. The social workers tried to rehabilitate him with his mother, but this failed. She would either fail to turn up or arrive drunk. 'Emotionally, he'd switched off,' said Wendy. They gave up trying to reunite him with his mother when he was fifteen months old. 'When he came to us, he had that look. He's never, even now at twenty four, never come out from behind those eyes. As a toddler, he never cried or smiled. He would go off with anyone. He'd put up his little hand and go off with whoever it was.' After the age of three he refused to be kissed by Wendy. 'He even took that away from me. He played and he was curious but he did not really relate.'

For some, not only was there emotional distance but also emotional suppression. Physical hurt and injury would rarely elicit tears or require comfort. feelings would be controlled and there would a determination not to be helped or affected by other people. Giles 'would never cry, no matter how badly hurt or injured he was,' his mother said. He seemed to look in on the family, but from a distance:

'The bonding has always been a problem with Giles. We've been there, but he's circled round us. It's still the case. The circles could be quite close, like when he was young, or miles away, like when he was in his late teens. He'd live a few miles away, and visit the house but not let us know he was there. He never wanted cuddles. If he hurt himself, he never bothered. He's had the most tremendous accidents, but he would never cry. And later, say if we were in church, he'd deliberately separate himself from us. We'd be in the front and he would be right at the back. Same when we went to America. In the airport lounge, he'd know where we were but we didn't know where he was. And he wouldn't sit near us on the aeroplane.'

Few friends

Emotional distance and self-control affected sociability. Throughout most of their childhoods, these children had few close friends. Parents would often describe them as "loners". Some children behaved aggressively, even viciously, when they were playing with age-mates. They found it hard to enter the "give-and-take" of relationships. Not surprisingly, these children were not popular. They seemed to lack empathy and social competence. Some were bullies.

Fiona felt that both Polly and Neil were socially very poor:

'They were not very good with other children. They'd quarrel and push and squabble and scratch. If they didn't get their own way or wanted something that somebody else had, it would always lead to a fight. So they didn't have any close friends. If another child did come round, I had to be there to supervise them. Polly preferred just one-to-one contact with an adult. This really carried on right into her late teens. When she started college on a YTS scheme she could never get on with the other students. She couldn't share. She said she was always being treated unfairly.'

School

Academic achievements were poor or non-existent. Social behaviour became so bad in adolescence in some cases that school was disrupted and often incomplete. These children had no sense of responsibility, either socially or educationally. Suspensions and expulsions were common. Teachers spoke critically and despairingly of these children. School reports would be poor and parents would dread attending parents' open evenings. The ability to concentrate was low. Many of the girls were in trouble for 'chatting too much and talking all the time'. They would 'not mind their own business' and get on with their own work. Mounting frustrations would regularly erupt into temper or violence. And those who were not particularly disruptive lacked motivation and just coasted along, essentially uninvolved. Truanting, especially in adolescence, was common.

Aged eleven, Giles transferred to the local senior day school. His behaviour had not improved. 'I used to dread one o'clock,' remembered Edna. 'The phone would ring and the school would say "Giles has gone". He truanted almost daily. He ended up with no qualifications.' By the time he was seven, the teachers began to lose patience with Giles. He would disrupt the class and demand to be the centre of attention. His parents then decided that he should board. He came home at weekends. 'It was when he was first away from home,' said Edna, 'that we realised how tense and worn out we had become. The tension reduced while he was away.' 'He didn't bother about being boarded,' Ted said. 'He thought it was great but he never worked.'

Martin

Martin, whose mother was white and father African-Caribbean, had spent many years in a children's home, before going to live with Joan. He kept getting into scrapes. 'He did silly things. He thought he'd start a fire in the waste paper basket and the school didn't like that much. He poured a bottle of ink into the goldfish pond and stained it blue. The staff were not impressed. One was beginning to hear phrases like, you know, "Martin is disruptive" and "Martin is underachieving."' Martin began to steal from Joan's purse when he was thirteen and this coincided with 'school being at an all time low'. At fourteen he was expelled. He was sent to a school for 'delicate children, but there was nothing delicate about Martin,' laughed Joan. 'He hated it. He was bright and he ran rings round them. He put all his energies into being a thorough nuisance. And things went from bad to worse. Everyone was going up the wall. And he was unhappy.'

Joan said she was so desperate, in the end she agreed with the social workers that he should go to an assessment centre:
  'It was awful. I didn't realise at first that I would have to sign him back into care. That was the worst thing I ever had to do. The case conference was a hideous experience for me. Everybody sat in a room and discussed my child while I sat outside. And I was never invited in. Anyway he was returned home. They said he had an IQ of 132. He went back to his old school. They kept him back a year and for a while everything went very well. But then when he was sixteen he stole £30 from another boy and he was expelled again. Possessions have always been important to Martin. And he's always been meticulously tidy. His room was spotlessly clean. But nevertheless, he left school with absolutely nothing.'

Adolescence and the further breakdown of relationships

The teenage years generally ushered in a phase of worsening behaviour. Relationships between parents and their children often reached breaking point. Schools found it difficult to cope with the increased disruptiveness. Lying became routine. Some children would go missing over night or run away for a day or two.

Unlike "angry" children, these more wary or uninvolved children did not personalise their aggression or direct it at their parents in particular. The *wary* children were emotionally *controlled* and distant. In contrast, the *uninvolved*, socially indiscriminate children were emotionally *uncontrolled*, disorganised and labile. This second group were impulsive, inattentive, immature, attention-seeking and ill-disciplined. Alan had experienced a highly disturbed, unsettled early childhood prior to his adoption. His teenage years were typical of the children found in this group.

Alan

For the first fifteen months of his life, Alan had been 'like a travelling parcel going from home to hospital to foster parents to nursery to hospital back to nursery and so on.' When he joined Mark and Beth, 'he was very passive. He never cried. Even if he hurt himself, he never cried.' When Beth told the social worker of this, the reply was, 'You ought to be glad you've got such a good child.' His odd behaviour began to be more apparent at the age of three. One night, Beth said to all three children, 'Let's have tea by the fire and watch TV.' The older two rushed excitedly into the kitchen and helped prepare the tea. 'But Alan put on his Wellington boots and coat. He went out into the dark in the garden and watched us through the window and wouldn't come in.'

When he reached the age of seven, he began to set fire to things. He started to soil himself. When he learned to ride his bike, he insisted on riding along a busy road on the wrong side. 'And if you told him it was very, very dangerous,' said Mark, 'he would just shrug.' 'It was this constant feeling we were not making any connection with him,' remembered Beth. By nine, he was stealing chocolate from the local shop and taking money from his parents. He was having therapy from the educational psychologist but his behaviour continued to get worse. As his stealing continued and he became more violent. Beth described the following incident:

> 'He must have been thirteen. He went missing one night. I went looking for him and eventually found him. But as I came towards him, he picked up a knife and he came towards me. He had that scary look in his eyes. I thought "If I don't get out now, he'll kill me." And he came with his knife looking very threatening and his eyes were completely empty. The girlfriend he was with was completely terrified. Her parents were out. And again, only a few weeks after this, he was at home and I simply went towards him and he threw me across the room. He said "You never wanted me". I was just one in a long line of women who hadn't wanted him, and I was no different to them as far as he was concerned. I was a woman who would let him down and he was driving me to make me let him down. We just couldn't reach him.'

Alan's school found it increasingly difficult to cope with him and he was eventually excluded. But at home his criminal and violent behaviour continued. 'We were on a slippery slope,' said Mark. 'Social workers and police were involved. He was in court, in prison, in a juvenile detention centre. But we stuck with him wherever he was.' His offences were always silly or petty – he broke into a police car and stole a "walkie-talkie", he took cars, he stole his landlord's cheque book. All his friends had left home and were also engaged in small-scale crime. 'Prison for Alan was like a womb,' thought Beth. 'All the strain went from his face. He almost blossomed. No decisions to make.' When he left prison, he chose to live a few miles away from his parents. Their relationship improved slightly. Alan is now twenty four and married; he dips in and out of their lives. Mark said:

> 'He's more settled. We started to talk openly about our feelings for one another. But then he suddenly upped and disappeared again. He crashes in and out of our lives. He springs up out of the blue. He has three children by two different women. At the moment he's crashed out and vowed to have nothing more to do with us ever again. We'll just have to wait and see.'

Leaving home

Children who had never really invested a great deal in their relationship with their parents and who seemed fairly indifferent and somewhat casual about maintaining closeness, would often leave home and lose contact. Initiatives tended to come from mothers and fathers. More than any other group, these children were likely to be unemployed. Marjorie and Kevin, both white adopters, still found themselves having to make all the running with Dee whose mother was black African-Caribbean and father white English, even though she was now twenty two years old. She had joined their family when she was five years old after several years in a children's home:

'She was absolutely lazy at home. Wouldn't lift a finger. She used to drive us to the limits as if she was trying to make us say "Go!". It's a good way of going if someone kicks you out. It's then our decision and not hers. I don't think she was happy here. I felt abused by her. At seventeen she went to live with her sister but after six months that broke down. Again, Dee didn't do a thing around the house. She then tried a number of lodgings and bed-sits. She pops in very occasionally. She's unemployed. With her it has been take, take, take all the time. There's no give. No emotional closeness, no practical help, no cards or presents. Still, there's time yet, I suppose.'

There is a final group who suddenly left and disappeared without warning. Martin, at the age of twenty four 'just disappeared into the blue'. Joan deduced that he had returned to one of his childhood towns. 'But it was ages before I heard from him. Five months later I got a letter and his phone number. He'd got a job as a security guard.'

Outcomes and looking back

The underlying insecurity that had so badly disturbed childhoods echoed into adulthood. Relationships with friends or intimate partners were volatile or short-lived. There was a lack of trust in other people and a feeling that life was against them. A few had managed to hold down steady jobs, but many found themselves in and out of work. Some were sacked from job after job. Others left because of a row or felt that they were being exploited or used in some way. Food preparation, catering and working with vulnerable groups were the most common lines of work taken, partly because these were relatively easy types of employment to find, but partly because people had a particular interest in looking after little children or working with food.

Although things were uniformly grim throughout adolescence, two broad types of outcome were discernible by the time the adopted children had reached their early to mid-twenties: parents had lost contact with their grown-up child, or parents had intermittent but improving contact with their grown-up child.

Some parents had either lost or cut off contact with their child. A history of rows, violence and dishonesty had proved too much for mothers and fathers. There was no wish to return to a difficult and highly stressful relationship. Millie and Rob's time with Dale had been an unhappy one. He left home at sixteen.

'He wanted to be a motor mechanic but kept getting the sack, job after job. He then started stealing cars, going to court and we reached an all time low. I said "This is it, Dale". He's now twenty two and we've had no contact with him for over a year now. He never fitted into our family [four birth children and three adopted children]. To be quite honest, I think he's a bit of a bounder. He always seemed to have a big chip on his shoulder. Lots of moans. Things would start off fine, but they would go wrong. He was a bully and he was dishonest. I was always trying to reach him, but I never did.'

For other parents and their children there was a slow, hesitant improvement in relationships. Contact might be intermittent or exploratory, but both children and parents wished to hold on to and develop the emerging trust and intimacy. In these cases, it seemed that the children, after almost twenty years, were just beginning to feel that the relationship was secure and reliable. They were beginning to share bits of themselves with their mothers or fathers. Parents were pleased at the small progress and were realising how emotionally damaged their children had been during their first few years of childhood. They were touched by the clumsy and transparent attempts to get close.

Garth

Garth, a black boy of African-Caribbean parents, went to the local college to do a catering course. 'He did extremely well,' said Bruce, his white adoptive father, 'but we didn't know he did extremely well until a long time after because he never told us anything. This was Garth doing it all himself again, being independent, you see.' After qualifying, Garth, by sheer persistence, managed to get himself a job in a prestigious restaurant. However, his successes in this field appeared to have given him confidence and after various extra studies, he was offered a job working for the government. At the age of twenty four he is half way through completing a part-time economics degree. 'He has met the most splendid girl who has helped him enormously,' said Evelyne, 'helped him work things out. The last couple of years, I think he's thought a lot of things through. He's been to see our parents. He seems to be beginning to "own" us and our family, I think. He comes home now with friends and actually introduces us for the first time as "Mum and Dad". And he's just changed his name legally to incorporate our surname with his. We're just starting to get birthday cards and Christmas presents. He's even brought his girlfriend to meet us. We keep chalking up firsts even though he's twenty four!'

The difficult behaviour of these more detached and uninvolved children, unlike their "angry" counterparts, was less personalised and not directed at their parents. Although adopters were often disappointed with these less giving children, in an odd way, they felt less traumatised than some of the parents of "angry" children. Again, though, parents who did manage to stay with the children into early adulthood began to see signs of their children trying to get closer. These were the least socially accomplished or competent children. It took most of them until their twenties even to begin to feel a growing sense of trust and security in family life. In spite of all that had happened, their parents still appeared to be available. This acted as a powerful emotional message. This constancy, this willingness not to give up, slowly, very slowly allowed the children to explore ways of getting closer. It helped them learn of the attractions and emotional benefits of social intimacy.

10 Birth mothers, biology and beliefs

Although most parents soon lost any feelings of self-consciousness about having children by adoption, nevertheless, in most cases the adoptive dimension remained real and relevant. This did not mean that adoption as such was viewed negatively or that it intruded itself inappropriately. Rather, for most parents and their children it was something that cropped up as an interesting and relevant matter from time to time. Children naturally asked about their background and origins. There was curiosity about birth mothers and fathers. When all was going well and relationships between parents and children were comfortable, discussions about adoption would be useful and relaxed. However, if there were stresses and insecurities, talk about adoption would be more tense and loaded.

In this final chapter, mothers and fathers talk about aspects of parenting which are special and peculiar to adoption. From the parents' point of view, these distinctive features revolve around the birth mother and father on the one hand and the needs and behaviour of adopted children on the other. Birth parents, biological and genetic issues, and support and personal beliefs reveal some of the experiences that are unique to adoptive parents.

Birth parents

It was not at all unusual for adoptive mothers to admit that the birth mother remained as a "presence" throughout the adoption. Adopters would think and wonder about her. Her "presence" was not necessarily threatening or disconcerting (although it could be) but there was an understanding that another woman existed who was also the mother of the adopted child. Indeed, without this other woman's pregnancy, the adoptive parents would not be parents, at least as far as that particular child was concerned. There appeared to be no obvious correlation between the slight anxieties experienced by some adoptive parents and their child's feelings of security. Sandra had adopted two children, now both grown up:

'You can never quite get out of your head the poor girl who gave them up and what she's missed. For example, I've now got these two beautiful granddaughters and it occurred to me that there's this other woman and she's got these granddaughters as well. It's a slightly odd feeling.'

Elaine adopted Oliver when he was three months old. For both mother and son, the birth mother continued to be an absent third party in their relationship:

'Oliver had a habit of saying things out of the blue. When he was seven, he suddenly said, "When I get bullied I wish I could go to my other mother." This was a bit of a bombshell at quarter-to-nine in the morning. But it showed me that his mother was a fantasy of safety for him. His mother has been very important in his life and all our lives. Again, when he started secondary school, he said, "Do you think she'll be thinking of me today?" She was always there for him. I suppose I must have conveyed things to him. I would say things like "I wish she could know how well you're doing at school." I mean, I didn't overdo it but she never really was out of mind. I always thought of him as hers and mine. And because it was natural for me to think about her, I wish I had met her.'

It was mainly adoptive mothers who spoke of the birth mother. Their feelings towards her ranged widely. Some were grateful to her, others wanted her to know how well her son or daughter had done in life. When Stella walked down the street 'with this beautiful baby in the pram,' she had fantasies that every young woman she passed might be Philip's mother: 'I wanted her to see him. I cried the day he went to school. "If only you could see him now," I thought. And it was the same at his graduation. All those high days and holidays when I was I was so proud of him and I wanted her to see him.'

Other adopters, though, said their peace of mind was slightly unsettled by the birth mother's continued existence. They felt tinges of insecurity. Although rationally they knew there was no real question to whom their child belonged, occasionally parents worried and fantasised that this other mother might somehow reclaim their child, or their son or daughter might suddenly decide that they would prefer to live with their birth mother.

Some parents were very keen that their children, when old enough, should search for their birth mother and actively encouraged their children to make enquiries. However, in most cases, although the adoptive parents were morally supportive, they admitted that the idea of their son or daughter meeting their birth mother caused them to feel a little anxious and frightened. 'What if Karen prefers her to me? I know she loves me, but there's that silly doubt.' Lena said her husband was much more relaxed than she felt about her daughter searching:

'This tracing business worries me quite a bit. There's a bit of me that can't get Susie's birth parents out of my mind. My dread is that if Susie found her natural parents she might say "I've found my parents. You're not my parents." I don't think that would ever really happen, but I suppose I fear the hurt.'

A few parents even expressed feelings of guilt. The birth mother's misfortune was their happiness; her pain was the cause of their joy.

Those who had adopted older children expressed a different range of emotions. The children had been adopted usually after a history of neglect or abuse. Incompetent and inadequate parents usually earned the sympathy of the adopters. The struggles, stresses and strains that many birth parents suffered were appreciated. However, many adopters found it hard to forgive birth parents who had either physically or sexually abused their children. These feelings were roused most strongly when social workers had insisted on contact being maintained between children and their birth mothers and fathers. This was most likely to happen if the child was fostered initially.

Telling

All the parents told their children at some stage during their childhood that they were adopted. In most cases, adoption workers had provided parents with ideas and advice about how to tell their son or daughter that they were adopted. The parents' levels of confidence affected how relaxed they felt discussing adoption with their children. The more at ease with the notion of adoption were the parents, the more matter-of-fact about their adoption were the children. Parents revealed a huge range of techniques for telling children about their adoption. Most introduced the notion from quite a young age. The child's "adoption story" – how they came to join the family – was a great favourite with many young children. Dyllis had an adoption story for Lisa:

'When she was three, I was putting her to bed one night and she asked for her story which we were told to give a positive aspect. On this occasion, though, she threw me. She asked "Why did they give me away?" She used to romanticise who she was. She was always curious about her mother. She actually started searching when she was in her twenties, but she stopped when she got pregnant. I confess, I was a bit uneasy about her finding this woman although I knew it was the natural thing to do. But in spite of me knowing it was right and proper, I couldn't stop myself feeling a little hurt.'

Although most adoption stories were relatively easy to tell and could be given a positive connotation without too much difficulty, one or two parents of children adopted as babies had slightly more difficult tales to relate. If a mother had committed suicide or a birth father had murdered the birth mother, adopters had little choice in these early years but to gloss over some of the more painful details. Louise was never quite sure whether to believe that her mother had actually abandoned her. In her teens she could sometimes feel anger towards her. Eileen, Louise's adoptive mother, had taken her back to the Philippines a few times to visit the beach where she was found and the orphanage where she was first taken. Eileen said:

'I could identify with this poor birth mother's pain. She was young, poor and desperate. I told Louise all about her history. I tried to get her to see things positively. Instead of saying that she was "abandoned" on a beach, I would say "placed on a beach in order to be found". She used to call herself a "beach-babe with class". While other girls would say that they were born in such a hospital, she would say "Well, I was born under the stars on a beach". You must admit it sounds wonderfully exotic and romantic!'

Parents varied a great deal in how they handled the matter of adoption once it had been told. Some preferred not to mention it again, unless their children insisted on raising it. However, if children sensed it was a matter of some anxiety or discomfort for their parents, they tended not to mention it, at least with their mothers or fathers. Most parents, though, discussed it as and when it cropped up. It was not a topic of constant conversation, but they seemed happy to sit and talk about it in a comfortable and interested fashion if it seemed of passing interest to their children. Odd or unexpected incidents would trigger a discussion – a lesson on genetics at school, a programme on television featuring an adopted person, the adolescent child being in reflective mood.

A few parents attempted to build in more regular reminders of their child's adoptive status. The intention was both to acknowledge the adoption and give it a positive spin. Whether or not the strategy was successful or appropriate was not always clear. Meg and Ray marked Andy's arrival as his "adoption day", which, like his birthday, involved the giving of presents. 'We did it just to keep the word "adoption" in his mind. Until he was about eight or nine, Andy thought everyone was adopted and that adoption was the norm.'

Although most parents followed professional advice and chose not to mention that their son or daughter was adopted unless it seemed either appropriate or relevant to mention it (which was rare), a couple of parents decided that it would be a good thing whenever they met someone new, to introduce their children as 'This is my adopted son, Paul,' or 'This is Jane, my adopted daughter.' Penny said that she had read a great deal about adoption. 'We decided that we were going to tell them right from the beginning so that they would grow up in the full knowledge that they were adopted. We would introduce them as our adopted son and daughter and add "isn't it wonderful!" so that it never became a big issue.'

Children placed at an older age, of course, often had clear memories of their parents, first family and home. A lot would depend on how the children remembered these earlier years, but most adopters had no doubts that this phase of their children's lives required clear, full and honest acknowledgement. Contact with birth parents was sometimes maintained through photographs, occasional letters and even, in a few cases, through actual contact. In earlier chapters, we have heard adopters describe the success or otherwise of these contacts. Some were effective and adopters spoke positively of the practice. But equally, a number of parents felt their children's meetings with their birth mothers or fathers were upsetting, disturbing and not to be recommended.

By the time the children reached adolescence, the full meaning and nature of adoption was apparent. Depending on individual children's temperament, experience of adoption and perception of their parent's degree of comfort with the topic, four attitudes could be struck concerning their adoption:

- relaxed, secure and interested;
- neutral and allegedly uninterested;
- anxious and definitely *not* interested; and
- anxious, angry and preoccupied with the reasons for being adopted in the first place.

The first group of children were relaxed and naturally curious about their origins and birth parents. They were secure in their relationships with their adoptive parents and knew they could discuss adoption at any time if they wanted to. Many of these children, though by no means all, went on to search for information about their birth parents or made contact with them. This usually received the full backing and support of their parents. Indeed, it was not unusual for adopted children to ask their mothers to help them search and check things out. The adopters' relationship was never threatened by the contact and although mothers and fathers might feel twinges of anxiety, the children were never in any doubt that their adoptive parents were and always would be "mum and dad". When Gill was a girl she would wonder what her birth mother looked like. 'So I told her to look in the mirror,' said Edith. 'When Gill was in her late twenties she did meet her mother. In fact all three of us met up on one occasion and Gill said "My two mums!" and she put her arms round us. It went off very well, really. She keeps in touch with her mother from time to time, but Gill and the grandchildren live just down the road from us. She's made us very, very happy.'

The reunions with birth parents ranged from the successful in which both sets of parents and their children formed positive relationships through to those which petered out once the children's curiosity had been satisfied. A few caused upset. Birth mothers might lose interest or refuse to see their children. Relationships between them and their birth children might not work out, and contact would end on an unsatisfactory note. Gina traced her birth mother when she was twenty. 'They arranged to meet,' said her adoptive mother, Adina, 'and I felt terrible. I worried that the mother might have tried to reclaim her. Anyway, they met for a couple of hours but Gina felt relieved when I returned. She didn't enjoy the contact. She said "Oh Mummy, I'm glad you're back. She didn't even offer me any lunch. She showed me around her house as if I was a visitor and didn't really belong to her." She was very disappointed.' But just as often, adopters reported, often with relief, that the reunion had gone well, their children still saw them as mum and dad, and life continued as before.

The second group claimed not to be interested in their birth parents. 'You're my mum and dad, and that's fine by me. So, no need to talk about it.' These children entered adulthood in contented mood, never express-ing much curiosity about their adoption. They rarely thought about searching, at least in their younger years. In some cases, however, it tran-spired that the children sensed that their parents still had underlying fears and anxieties about the birth mother. Loving and feeling protective towards their parents, they suppressed any interest in their background. They felt that if they did search, it would upset their mothers and fathers and this they very much did not want to do. However, one or two children did carry out covert searches, mainly out of natural curiosity. And although they were right to suspect that their parents would be hurt when eventually they did learn of the contact, the upset was as much to do with not telling them as meeting the birth mother. The outcome generally wit-nessed a happy conclusion for all parties. The fears of the adopters were allayed; the curiosity of the children was satisfied; and the birth parents enjoyed learning about the successes of their long-ago relinquished children. There was never any doubt in the children's minds that their adoptive parents were still "mum and dad", but the contact did allow them to complete the story of their lives – they had a full understanding of who they were and from where they had come. Ruby described how she felt when her daughter Debbie found her birth mother:

'Debbie found her birth mother. At the time it really upset me. We were the last to know. She was twenty four. She told her friends but she said she was too frightened to tell us. She had counselling first. Then she got in touch with her mother. I was very, very hurt. She was frightened we were going to turn her out. But of course, that's the very last thing we would ever do. She found her birth mother in Darlington and went to see her. She said to her that she didn't want another mother but she wanted to know her background before starting a family of her own. She was very curious. We invited Debbie's mother to her wedding and we got on fine. She's a very nice, quiet woman. I was very apprehensive. I was very upset, though, when Debbie went up to Darlington. I didn't know what might happen. They keep in touch a bit, but there's not much contact now. She's satisfied her curiosity. And my goodness, they aren't half alike! Now, looking back, I'm glad she did find her. It seems to have satisfied her.'

The third group was made up of children who actively opposed any discussion about their adoption. In their teens, they would walk out of the room if a brother or sister wanted to talk about their birth parents. Any television programme about adoption would be switched off or the children would leave. 'Alex got really irritated if anyone ever mentioned adoption,' said Elsa. 'He'd say that there was only one proper mum and dad and he really did not want to talk about his natural mother. He didn't mind quite so much us mentioning where he was born, but any mention of mothers or fathers and he would be off.' It was unusual for these children, even as young adults, to think about making any enquiries of their background or birth parents. Glen told Shirley, his mother, that 'If she [his birth mother] rejected me as a baby, then I don't see why I should want to have anything to do with her.'

The final group were much more confused and angry. They were either very hostile towards their birth mother or angry with their adoptive parents or both. 'Karleen could never forgive her mother for rejecting her,' said Mo. 'She would say things like "That bitch didn't want me and you're hopeless too." She got very mixed up and agitated in her teens.' Some children vowed never to make contact with their birth mother and yet remained absorbed in the meaningfulness to them of her original decision to place them for adoption. Others chose to search for her, usually in quite an aggressive mood, during their late teens or early twenties. Finding information about or meeting the birth mother often had the effect of 'laying a ghost to rest'. The contact calmed the adult adopted person. This did not necessarily mean that the reunion went well. Some meetings were successful but it was just as likely that having made contact, the child lost all interest in the birth parent who could be left emotionally high and dry. In both cases, there was usually an improvement in the relationship between the children and their adoptive parents. It was as if the unfinished business of the initial rejection was finally completed and life could resume where it had left off.

Biology: genes and upbringing

Nearly all parents began the adoption firmly believing that it was the quality of care rather than the power of genes that would wholly determine their children's development. Twenty or more years later, only a few still retained a firm belief that the way their children turned out was entirely down to their upbringing and they were responsible, as parents, for all that was either good or bad in their children.

By the time the children reached adulthood, most parents said that they realised that many of their children's prime characteristics and personality traits were either inborn or inherited. This belief in the significant part that genes play seemed to be confirmed if children found their birth parents and the adopters also met them. 'She was just like her mother. Uncanny really.' This was usually said with a smile. When Melanie took her mother, Shula, along to meet her birth father, it struck Shula how alike they both were. Melanie was easy going, very likeable and kind-hearted. 'He was a very laid-back West Indian guy,' said Shula. 'A lovely man and very relaxed. I think people have given too much weight to nurture. I think nature has more of a say in the way we turn out.'

As far as Beattie was concerned, 'heredity wins over environment, no doubts.' She was adopted herself, but she and her husband felt that 'although environment is important, heredity predominates.' Over the years, Marjorie had totally switched her views on the influence of family life:

'Before I had a baby, I had very definite ideas that given a tiny, wee child – a baby – with all the love and facilities and sense, you could bring up a star. You could make a baby into anything you wanted to. Now I could convince anybody that actually you have very little ability to change very much! What they are is what they are!'

None of this was to deny that the adopters did not have any influence, but it did indicate that most parents of adopted babies started off with a fierce belief in the primacy of upbringing and a strong rejection of the idea that genes and biology would have a significant impact on the development of *their* child. If the adoption had worked out well – and most baby adoptions *did* work out well – the parents' love and pride in their children meant that they could feel more relaxed and easy about the part that inheritance played. They conceded that some basic features of their children's make-up, including temperament, personality and intelligence, seemed to come with them and were not learned. Ironically, if things had not worked out so well, parents often blamed the competence of their parenting and not the quality of their children's genes.

The effect of genes, at least as far as parents believed, expressed themselves in three areas of their children's' lives:

- mannerisms, interests, talents, temperament and personality;
- temperaments and behaviours which were similar to those of their birth parents; and
- jobs, skills and careers which were similar to those of their birth parents.

If adoptive parents also had birth children, they could make comparisons. Some saw no difference and simply concluded that each child was different and adoption did not come into it. Others felt they detected family resemblances in the biologically related children. June felt that Richard had a different set of talents to his brothers and sisters:

'Of course each of my children are different in their own way, but I think we have . . . I mean I can see a strain going through all of us, the birth children, that leans towards the arty world and the sort of imaginative, creative, inner kind of thing, you know, stories, poetry, drama, acting, that sort of thing. Richard was always more interested in maths and physics. Never stories or the arts.'

It seemed uncanny to some adoptive mothers and fathers that their children should choose careers and occupations that were the same as those of one of their birth parents. Several daughters of nurses went into nursing; a son whose birth father was a journalist became a writer; a daughter who was very good at horse-riding discovered that her birth mother was a point-to-point champion. In the eyes of adopters, this seemed to clinch the power of genes over environment:

'One of the things which I thought was really interesting was how from a very early age Sarah would preen herself in front of the mirror. She would dress up in my clothes and high heels, put on lipstick, all kinds of beauty things and I used to smile because I never look in a mirror and I always look tatty. I thought she's obviously not inherited that from me. It must be from her natural mother who – would you believe – was a beauty therapist! There must be something in the genes that makes her want to be interested in what she looks like.'

Parents who adopted a child of a different race had to cope with the difference of skin colour and, with older placed children, cultural differences. Examples of bringing up a child transracially have been mentioned throughout earlier chapters. In this section, I want to highlight some of the experiences of both parents and children. Although some parents said that they did not think that their child had suffered any racism, the majority recognised that for their black children, racism was a regular and major part of their experience. The backwash of racism was also felt by parents. As mother and fathers of a black child they found themselves on the receiving end of some very hostile views. 'When Angeline was a toddler,' said Veronique, 'people would say to me "What are you doing with a black bastard." The racism I encountered was extraordinary.' Even minor incidents revealed the odd and ignorant attitudes of many white people. 'Most people were very pleased and supportive when Will arrived,' said Christine. 'But we did have some weird things said to us. One old lady down the road said to me "What are you going to do with him when he starts talking. You won't understand what he's saying." '

And as white parents of a black child, they had a glimpse of how the world appeared to a young black person. When sons and daughters came

137

home from school and reported racially motivated insults and attacks, they had an insight into what life was like for their children. Connie remembered walking home with Greg from junior school:

'He'd be walking along, holding my hand. He'd see the youngsters who shouted "nigger" at him when he was at school. He'd immediately drop my hand and he'd walk by me absolutely independently. He was frightened but he handled it very well.'

Alice was so upset and angry when she learned that her young African-Caribbean daughter was being taunted that she decided to educate Rachel privately:

'When she was six, she got teased a lot at school because of her colour. She'd come home and say "Mummy, nobody will hold hands with me when we're playing." Twice she came home and asked me to disinfect her mac because she had been spat at. I tackled the school over this but they seemed unable to do much about it. She was the only black child in the school. I withdrew her and sent her to a private tutor and she flourished.

'I did send her to secondary school but there was more racism there. She was called a nigger and told that niggers belonged in the gutter. The school told me to stop complaining. They said it was my fault. They said I should help Rachel get a thicker skin. So I transferred her to my own school which I started first of all for two of the younger children. Rachel finished her schooling with me and got three 'O' levels. When she left, she helped me for a while in the junior and senior school before she eventually trained as a nursing auxiliary.'

Belief and support

Having children by adoption is different. Parents recognised this difference in a myriad of little ways as they talked about their children. But difference does not mean better or worse; it simply means that in some respects having your children by adoption requires parents and children to acknowledge such differences. For most parents this was an easy thing to do. The adoption was talked about from time to time in a comfortable and confident manner. Birth parents were discussed, and in some cases contact was made with them in adult life, often with the support of the adopters. These were happy and successful adoptions. Looking back, parents expressed much love for and pride in their children.

However, a small number of children, particularly those placed as toddlers and older who had been neglected and looked after in an inconsistent manner before their adoption, could not adjust to being adopted. They could not get over the fact that their birth mother had given them up. They remained preoccupied with this early rejection and continued in a state of agitation and anger throughout much of their childhood. These children were less easy to look after. Parents' patience and resolve were often tested to the limit. Looking back, these parents were often ambivalent about the adoption. If the children eventually calmed down and stopped being angry, reconciliations were possible and the adoption was reviewed as ultimately worthwhile. But if the grown-up child continued to be hostile or difficult, it was less easy for mothers and fathers to look back on the adoption with much satisfaction. However, there were many exceptions. Some parents managed to deal with children whose behaviour was very difficult and disturbed without losing hope. They expected little from their children and were pleased at the slightest progress. When they looked back, they were realistic and forgiving. They saw the adoptions as successful. And because they viewed their children and their adoption in a positive light, it seemed that the children responded accordingly. Parental belief in the potential of their children coupled with an optimistic outlook brought their own rewards.

Adopters gained support from many quarters. The family itself could be a strength and a resource. Two mothers whose husbands had died said how tremendously caring and supportive their children had been at the time of the loss. 'Peter's death has certainly kept us all very close to one another,' said Joseline. Parents of large families described how older brothers and sisters would help out not only practically but emotionally too. Older placed children, wary of too much intimacy, sometimes latched on to a big sister or grown-up brother. 'A lot of our success with these disturbed children,' believed Alice, 'is not to do with Donald or me but the other children. We often took a back seat when a new child arrived. It's the others that made them feel at home.'

Grandparents, friends and other adopters were also sources of support and understanding. The more difficult and demanding children placed stresses and strains on marriages and family life. It was important for parents to be able to talk matters over with people who understood.

A significant number of adopters said that they found their faith helped them through some of the more trying times. And if their church or religion also offered social support, this was a double bonus. 'We are Christians,' said Elaine, 'and the strength of our own faith helped us through some difficult times. And the church backed us too. Lots of people were very supporting and prayed for us.' Peggy, who had raised five older placed children, was in the Salvation Army and her faith had been and still was very important to her:

'The Army has been good to me. I have support from my faith and my friends. I have people I can moan to! I couldn't have done any of this without the Lord or without prayer or the support of friends in the Army. I am a firm believer that God does not give us any more than we can carry.'

Help from professionals was seen as less reliable. Although many individual counsellors, lawyers, adoption specialists and post-adoption agencies were described as being particularly helpful, the general feeling was that more run-of-the-mill experts in children's behaviour were not very good. The accusation was that many psychologists, psychiatrists and social workers failed to understand or take into account the special character of being an adopted child or an adoptive parent. Assessments seemed woefully off-target. Treatments were described as ineffective. And the parents very often felt blamed and scapegoated.

Belief remained important for parents of adopted children – belief in their children, belief in their abilities as parents, and belief in the value of not giving up and staying involved. With the growing need to place older children with disturbed backgrounds with new families, there is no doubt that adoptive parenting requires some of these beliefs to be present in strong measure. It also has to be admitted that although families were good for children whose behaviour was disturbed, such children were not always good for families.

With some exceptions, adopting babies was generally experienced as a success story. Parents looked back on their children's lives with pleasure and pride. Children who were adopted with a history of earlier family relationships and adverse experiences behind them generally demanded more of their new parents. These children had lost trust in the adult world and they were not about to commit themselves to new relationships without a good deal of caution and suspicion. Those parents who were able to stick with their children through the bad times as well as the good, felt that in the end their patience and staying power were rewarded. They often had to wait longer than other parents for their "success" but the happy ending seemed all the sweeter for that.

Some children whose behaviour was very disturbed did prove too difficult for parents. Although relationships between these children and adopters often broke down during adolescence, mothers and fathers recognised that their children's needs were so great that they understood the nature of some of the problems even if they no longer had the resources or strength to do much about them. They still retained feelings of love and concern for their children. Certainly, there was sadness at the way things had worked out. In a few cases there was even regret that the adoption had ever taken place. But looking back over the years, even with these children, there was recognition that some experience of a warm, loving family life had helped a little. It took a very long time for these children to mellow and develop trust. However, even in the most tense and stressful relationships there were reconciliations.

All children need to grow up in warm, loving, two-way relationships. When biological parents and families are unable to provide children with such relationships, it is up to others to provide them. It is testimony both to adopters and the healing power of good quality relationships that so many children whose lives began in adversity should grow up into mature, competent and able adults. Relationships with parents last a lifetime. They remain of fundamental importance to children whose lives have been transformed by the opportunity to love and be loved. The adopter's story is ultimately an uplifting tale of love which is unconditional, care which is warm, and commitment which is lifelong.

Useful organisations

British Agencies for Adoption and Fostering (BAAF)
BAAF is a registered charity and professional association for all those working in the child care field. BAAF's work includes: giving advice and information on aspects of adoption, fostering and child care issues; publishing a wide range of books, training packs and leaflets as well as a quarterly journal; providing training and consultancy services to social workers and other professionals to help them improve the quality of medical, legal and social work services to children and families; giving evidence to government committees on subjects concerning children and families; responding to consultative documents on changes in legislation and regulations affecting children in or at risk of coming into care; and helping to find new families for children through BAAF*LINK* and *Be My Parent*.

More information about BAAF can be obtained from:

Head Office
Skyline House
200 Union Street
London SE1 0LX
Tel. 0171 593 2000

Scottish Centre
40 Shandwick Place
Edinburgh EH2 4RT
Tel. 0131 225 9285

Welsh Centre
7 Cleeve House
Lambourne Crescent
Cardiff CF4 5GJ
Tel. 01222 761155

Central Region
St George's House
Coventry Road
Coleshill
Birmingham B46 3EA
Tel: 01675 463998

Northern Region
Grove Villa
82 Cardigan Road
Leeds LS6 3BJ
Tel. 0113 2744797

and at:

MEA House
Ellison Place
Newcastle upon Tyne
NE1 8XS
Tel. 0191 261 6600

Southern Region
200 Union Street
London SE1 0LX
Tel. 0171 928 6085

and at:

9 Stokes Croft
Bristol BS1 3PL
Tel. 0117 9425881

Be My Parent
200 Union Street
London SE1 0LX
Tel. 0171 593 2060/1/2/3

BAAF*LINK*
MEA House
Ellison Place
Newcastle upon Tyne
NE1 8XS
Tel. 0191 232 3200

Parent to Parent Information on Adoption Services (PPIAS)
PPIAS is a national organisation for adoptive parents, their children and those hoping to adopt. There are over 140 volunteer co-ordinators scattered throughout the country and most of these hold meetings where a wide variety of topics related to adoption.

PPIAS produces a quarterly journal, *Adoption UK*, full of fascinating experiences of adopters and adopted people. They also provide a range of further information packs and leaflets on specific topics and have a Resource Bank through which adopters can share similar experiences.

Parent to Parent Information on Adoption Services
Lower Boddington
Daventry
Northants NN11 6YB
Tel. 01327 260295

The National Organisation for Counselling Adoptees and their Parents (NORCAP)
NORCAP is a support group that offers the opportunity to talk to people who have had similar experiences. NORCAP aims to help and counsel: adopted people who are thinking of searching for their birth parents, birth parents who either long for, or dread, a contact from the past – they can be put in touch with others in the same position; adoptive parents whose lives will be affected by any search their adopted children may start.

NORCAP
112 Church Road
Wheatley
Oxon OX33 1LU
Tel. 01865 875000

Post and After Adoption Centres
There are many well established after adoption services now that provide a service for adoptive families, adopted people and birth parents whose children were adopted. Many of them offer counselling, preferably in person, but also on the telephone or by correspondence, for individuals and families.

Post-Adoption Centre
5 Torriano Mews
Torriano Ave
London NW5 2RZ
Tel. 0171 284 0555

After Adoption
12–14 Chapel Street
Salford
Manchester M3 7NN
Tel. 0161 839 4930

After Adoption
Yorkshire & Humberside

80–82 Cardigan Road
Leeds LS6 3BJ
Tel. 0113 2302100

After Adoption Wales
Unit 1 Cowbridge Court
58–62 Cowbridge Road
West Cardiff CF5 5BS
Tel. 01222 575711

West Midlands Post-Adoption Service (WMPAS)
92 Newcombe Road
Handsworth
Birmingham B21 8DD
Tel. 0121 523 3343

Merseyside Adoption Centre
316–317 Coopers Building
Church Street
Liverpool L1 3AA
Tel. 0151 709 9122

Adoption Counselling Centre
Family Care
21 Castle Street
Edinburgh EH2 3DN
Tel. 0131 225 6441

Barnardo's Scottish Adoption Advice Centre
16 Sandyford Place
Glasgow G3 7NB
Tel. 0141 339 0772

Useful reading

Chennels P, and Hamond C, *Adopting a Child: a guide for people interested in adoption*, BAAF, 1995.
Essential reading for anyone who is considering adopting a child, this down-to-earth guide gives clear and up-to-date information on all stages of the adoption process. It includes names and addresses of adoption and fostering agencies throughout the country, and details of other organisations concerned with adoption.

Austin J, (ed) *Adoption: The inside story*, Barn Owl Books, 1985.
Written by adoptive parents, this book contains real-life stories covering the pleasures and pains of adoption today. The experiences of parents who have evolved successful ways of describing their children's pasts provide ideas and encouragement.

Surviving Five, Barnardo's, 1993.
This short and very readable book gives an insight into how one family coped with the different needs of a family of five brothers and sisters from introductions through the first year of placement.

Kay J, *The Adoption Papers*, Bloodaxe Books, 1991.
Jackie Kay was adopted transracially by a white Scottish couple. *The Adoption Papers* is a collection of poetry, the major part of which expresses the different viewpoints of the mother, the birth mother, and the daughter.

Wells S, *Within me, Without me*, Scarlet Press, 1994.
This collection of personal stories explores the experiences of mothers who have given up children for adoption.

BAAF Leaflets

Adoption – Some questions answered
Basic information about adoption – the process, procedures and important matters for consideration.

If You are Adopted
Answers to some of the questions adopted children ask, aimed at the children themselves. Includes information on tracing birth parents.

Talking about Origins
An outline of adopted children's need to be told about adoption and the law on access to birth certificates.

Intercountry Adoption – Some questions answered
Information on adopting a child from overseas, including procedures, legislation, and where to obtain advice and further information.

Adoption & Fostering

BAAF's quarterly journal, *Adoption and Fostering*, contains features, news and information on a wide variety of important child care issues, and provides an all-round perspective on current and new developments.

By My Parent

BAAF's bimonthly newspaper features children of all ages and backgrounds needing permanent new families right across the UK.

BAAF Publications Catalogue

Send an A5 stamped self-addressed envelope for our *free* catalogue which lists over 100 titles on adoption, fostering and child care to

BAAF Publications

Skyline House
200 Union Street
London SE1 0LX